ADVANCE

"Mike Stanford has brilliantly combined pragmatism with optimism in *Leadership Transition*. He realistically illustrates the pain that we normally feel as we confront setbacks, and even failures. But Stanford provides us with guides and frameworks that offer an uplifting way forward. He challenges us to dig deeply into our inner selves so we can make choices about our next steps in our leadership journeys. His depiction of the Leader's Compass is a breakthrough that helps making those choices, while not easy, grounded and energizing."

DOUGLAS A. READY
Senior Lecturer, MIT Sloan School of Management

"Leadership is more than a task. It is also a sharing at personal values of the story you want to tell and the difference you want to make. In *Leadership Transition*, Michael Stanford shows us how understanding ourselves helps us to lead others, whether you're leading a team of mountain guides in a 200-year-old organization, leading climbers up a mountain, or leading other leaders in a complex and confusing company. Use it as your own guide to personal growth, especially if you are on a challenging path."

OLIVIER GREBER
President, Compagnie des Guides, Chamonix

"*Leadership Transition* is a treasure trove of ideas and practices to help us engage with the personal challenges that taking on a significant leadership role can bring. Grounded in experience and illuminated by numerous case studies, Stanford's wise and compassionate text draws on contemporary psychological insights to offer effective ways to navigate transition and flourish. Coaches, leaders, and all who seek new stories to live by will benefit from this timely book."

GEOFF MEAD, PH.D.
Professor of Narrative Leadership, author of *Coming Home to Story: Storytelling Beyond Happily Ever After* and *Telling the Story: The Heart and Soul of Successful Leadership*

"Powerful and compelling! *Leadership Transition* reminds us that so much of the agony and ecstasy of corporate change is borne by individual leaders who are subjected to enormous pressure, who navigate between order and disorder, and who strive to maintain their sense of themselves as they struggle to satisfy conventional expectations, despite the many dangerous currents swirling around them. An intensely personal and well-crafted analysis of the soul of leaders and of leadership."

BILL FISCHER
Professor of Innovation, coauthor of *Virtuoso Teams, The Idea Hunter* and *Reinventing Giants*

"*Leadership Transition* engages us at the crucial crossroads of our discomfort and our hope for better. Leadership has no script, yet Mike Stanford leads us towards the relative certainty of knowing our own narrative so that we become better able to navigate change. This is a book for any leader who is ever at a loss for the way forward and a beautiful and helpful addition to the libraries of practitioners, coaches and educators."

DR. KATHERINE SEMLER
Coauthor of *Running On Empty*

"Captivating and insightful, *Leadership Transition* is an essential guide for navigating the tumultuous waters of leadership. Mike Stanford offers profound insights into the inner workings of the leader's mind during times of uncertainty through his exploration of scientific research, schools of psychology and the power of inner narratives. By diving into the essence of the Leader's Compass, Stanford provides leaders with invaluable tools for steering through challenges with clarity and purpose. A must-read for anyone embarking on a leadership journey."

YESIM ÖZLALE ÖNEN
Sabancı Holding Human Capital and Sustainability Group President

"Too often we fail to acknowledge the very deep and often painful emotional journey of leadership, a path with no map or compass to guide us. Through great personal wisdom, Mike Stanford has accomplished what very few scholars have. *Leadership Transition* answers the critical questions that any leader must answer – what difference do 1 want to make, what impact 1 you want to have, and what is the legacy 1 want to leave? *Leadership Transition* takes you beyond the superficial 'five key things you need as a leader' and provides you with something far more meaningful – a way to navigate the storms of leadership and personal growth. It will help you find your way back home."

RICK LASH
Coauthor of *Once Upon a Leader: Finding the Story at the Heart of Your Leadership*

Published by
LID Publishing
An imprint of LID Business Media Ltd.
LABS House, 15-19 Bloomsbury Way,
London, WC1A 2TH, UK

info@lidpublishing.com
www.lidpublishing.com

A member of:

BPR
businesspublishersroundtable.com

© Michael Stanford, 2024
© LID Business Media Limited, 2024

Printed and bound in Great Britain by Halstan Ltd
ISBN: 978-1-911687-81-8
ISBN: 978-1-911687-82-5 (ebook)

Cover and page design: Caroline Li

LEADERSHIP TRANSITION

HOW LEADERS TURN CHAOS INTO GROWTH

MICHAEL STANFORD

MADRID | MEXICO CITY | LONDON
BUENOS AIRES | BOGOTA | SHANGHAI

LEADERSHIP TRANSITION

CONTENTS

To Mom and Dad,
who gave us the opportunity to live good stories.

To Roxane and Antoine,
who taught me to see the beauty around every corner.

And to every leader
who wants to make the right kind of difference,
no matter how hard it might be.

ACKNOWLEDGEMENTS

I'll start my acknowledgements by thanking Laurence Calhoun and Richard Tedeschi, two monumental researchers in the field of post-traumatic growth. Much of the work in these pages was steered by their insights into how our most challenging, painful experiences can help us grow. I'll also thank the first two executives I met, early in the research, who described their leadership transitions using the language of trauma. Their stories shifted my doctoral research away from conventional leadership transitions to the territory of profound personal development. Their openness and honesty showed me how to be honest with my own transitional experience, and how to be just as honest with why I needed to explore the territory.

My doctoral cohort had a tremendous influence on the evolution of the research that is described in this book. James Traeger, our group supervisor and cofounder of Mayvin Ltd, encouraged me to dig ever deeper with his sharp and undying curiosity. Katherine Semler and Paul Stanley were wonderful companions during the doctoral years and became good friends along the way. I owe them both a debt of gratitude for helping me see things differently. Steve Marshall and Margaret Gearty both shaped the research in important ways, especially in its later stages. James, Katherine, Paul, Steve, Margaret, many thanks for how you steadied me and nudged me forward.

I first started to put the results of the research into practice while I was a senior partner in Korn's Ferry's leadership development team. I could not have wished for a better testing ground. There are too many impressive colleagues from my Korn Ferry days to mention, but I'll thank Paul van Katwyck for his quiet insight, Rick Lash for his patient playfulness, and Yesim Ozlale for her willingness to go ever deeper into how leadership can be a wonderful laboratory for personal growth. I'll also thank Brigitte Morel-Curran for her work in the world of CEO transitions, where she is a phenomenal force and remains a treasured colleague. Brigitte, Paul, Rick, Yesim, I know we've all gone on to new adventures but I'm happy that our paths crossed when they did. I am all the wiser for knowing you.

Meta de Boer and Bjorn Winiger have been constant explorers with me as the ideas in this book made their way into the world of leadership development. They've both improved the ways in which interesting theory became useful practice. Thanks Meta and Bjorn, for bringing your Strategist and your Dreamer into Magician territory.

To Rox and Antoine, my endless thanks for your patience, your love, and your ability to teach me about rich narrative-building, every single day of our lives together. You kept me close and steadied me during my most difficult days and throughout the writing of this book.

If I've directed my work toward leadership's best narratives, it's in part because you've both shown me how beauty is around every corner. To John Evans, my thanks for your quiet, steady support when I needed it most. To Dad, Joseph Stanford, you are a most wonderful teacher. Thanks for your wisdom, and special thanks for your review of an early manuscript of this work. It has benefited tremendously from your careful eye and your deep understanding of the territory.

Finally, I would like to thank all the clients I've worked with over 33 years in leadership development and especially over the past decade, when my work turned toward leadership transitions. Your openness, honesty and willingness to explore into the hidden corners has been a tremendous gift. Without your courage these pages would be empty.

ORIGIN STORIES

Life itself means to separate and to be reunited, to change form and condition, to die and to be reborn. It is to act and to cease, to wait and to rest, and then to begin acting again, but in a different way. And there are always new thresholds to cross.

- ARNOLD VAN GENNEP,
THE RITES OF PASSAGE

Over the course of 33 years working in the field of leadership development, I've heard some incredible stories. I've heard stories from leaders who've overcome what felt like insurmountable obstacles in the course of their work. And stories of leaders struggling to understand who they are and how they can maintain themselves in the face of all that is expected of them. I've heard stories of shining optimism and hope playing out in the theatre of leadership, and stories of anger and bitterness and lingering doubt because the cost of leadership is sometimes too much to bear.

I've also heard stories that have changed the course of my work and my life.

Leadership Transition began with one of those stories. I first heard it when I was in the early days of doctoral work on how leaders manage their transitions into new roles. I was going through my own leadership transition at the time, and I imagined that a practitioner's doctorate on the subject might help advance my thinking on what makes for a successful role change. It helped that a few of my colleagues had some academic expertise in leadership transitions. It also helped that some popular leadership self-help books claimed to tackle the territory. I read all of them, and felt I had a good understanding of how to navigate the stormy waters I was about to sail.

I thought I knew my organization well. I'd been in it for a long time. When I was asked to take on a new role, I felt up to the challenge. But though we were a small organization, we were archly political. After a good start with my new team, I began to struggle with how politically difficult my leadership work had become. My new role meant that I had to take on some challenging behaviours from a few powerful people. I wasn't clever or mature enough to manage the task well and, predictably,

I found myself having to make a choice between staying in my role or liking who I was. After a couple of years of trying to win a fixed match, I left.

The story of how hard it can be to do the right thing is a common one in leadership, but when I first experienced it, it didn't feel common at all. It felt terrible and painful and threatening. Once-friendly hallways became suddenly dangerous. Trusted relationships turned treacherous. Through my long struggle in this losing battle, I lost trust in how organizations work. I lost my faith that lasting positive human connection was possible in organizational life. I lost confidence in my ability to understand what was going on. The inner maps I'd been using to guide myself didn't work any more.

Trauma researchers write about how disruptive experiences shatter how we make sense of the world and how we organize ourselves to operate in it (*narrative* or *schema destruction*, in trauma terms – we'll get back to this). In trauma, confusion reigns. They also write about how disruptive experiences sabotage our ability to think our way out of the confusion (*sabotaging our narrative-creating capability*, again in trauma terms – we'll get back to this too). Trauma packs a twin punch: it destroys the load-bearing walls of how we think about the world, and it prevents us from building new ones. That's how I felt. I didn't understand what was happening; I couldn't really say who I was now that I wasn't who I used to be, and I had no sense of how a good story for my career and my life might unfold.

In the middle of all this, I met Ash. Ash was one of a handful of leaders with whom I connected when people who were familiar with my drama introduced me to people who were living similar stories. We connected to share our experiences, and maybe to find some comfort in the sharing. It was from Ash that I learned an important truth: *that any leadership transition is an important opportunity for personal exploration and profound growth.* It was Ash who sowed the seeds of another important realization that was to come months later: *that we can shape the chaos around us better when we've taken care of the chaos inside of us.*

Ash and I first met for a coffee at the Balzac, a small tearoom in a small Swiss town close to where we both live. After we settled in and I'd shared the headlines of my story with her, Ash told me about her brutal ten-year-old leadership battle with her old employer. Her relationship with the organization began when it convinced her to leave her government research role to join as a senior executive in one of their important functional teams. Ash's advanced expertise impressed the company's leaders and, after plenty of assurances that her work would be valued at the highest levels, Ash accepted their offer.

Ash took on her new role with all the professionalism and energy that she expected of herself. Soon, in the course of her work, she uncovered some practices that she believed put the company and its customers at risk. When she first flagged these practices, she was ignored. When she persisted, she found that her ability to do her work was being sabotaged by a few people higher in the hierarchy who seemed to value short-term performance over the hard work of maintaining safe and sustainable practices.

When I met Ash, she was seated with her back to the wall of the café, a few papers and empty coffee cups strewn on the table in front of her. She looked like she'd been there for a while, maybe taking some time before our meeting to review the many notes she'd scribbled down to try to make sense of her story. She was small, well-dressed and, I soon discovered, impressively articulate in the precise way that scientists can be. I imagined that she connected easily with serious senior business leaders. But she seemed nervous. I was nervous too. It's not easy to tell the story of your shame and confusion when you don't yet know how it ends.

When Ash described how a few of the leaders above her began to exclude her from activities that were necessary for her to do her job, her voice turned hard. It became the voice of a leader who was fighting a strange battle, trying to do what she was hired to do and unable to make sense of the forces in her way. I understood the reflex: her voice was my voice. Like me, Ash couldn't manoeuvre her way to a good conclusion. She was forced out of the organization that had worked so hard to hire her, and in the ten years since her departure she'd dedicated herself to holding the company accountable. It was an all-consuming task.

Toward the end of our conversation, I asked Ash how she'd describe the difficult work of making sense of her experience. How do you stay whole? How do you not let your leadership struggles overwhelm the parts of your life that have been going well?

"It's psychological torture," Ash said. "It's an assault on the soul."

Of course, leadership transitions aren't always an assault on the soul. They can, and should, be rich territory for growth, for self-expression, for feeling successful, for testing ourselves and for living a life that enables us to have a positive, lasting impact on our worlds. But such growth doesn't always come easily. Sometimes we need to work at it.

In the universe, there are things that are known, and things that are unknown, and in between there are doors.

- WILLIAM BLAKE

TYPES OF TRANSITION

Leadership Transition is a guide for leaders whose leadership work takes them into new and challenging territory. The purpose of this book is to help leaders at all levels, from board members to CEOs to younger leaders who are working their way up to positions of greater complexity, to step into their leadership challenges intending to grow. Our work in the pages to come is a work of exploration, since unknown territories, the territories that ancient mapmakers used to mark with the mysterious warning 'Here there be dragons!' are rich territories for self-discovery. Dragons test us, ask us important questions about who we are, why we are that way and what is most important to us. Slaying dragons is the mythological equivalent of the hard work of self-exploration that helps us grow into someone we like more, someone who is steady and resolute and who works from a place of deep self-understanding. The task of transitioning in our leadership work gives us plenty of dragons to slay.

Leadership Transition is also a work of hope. I've written it because even our most difficult leadership challenges can be testing grounds that lead to rich personal growth. The stories in the pages to come are stories of leaders who have emerged from their most difficult leadership experiences wiser, happier, more comfortable in their skin, and more confident that they are equal to whatever challenges lie ahead. The work describes that necessary journey through the often-uncomfortable challenges of leadership toward a deep sense of self-awareness and self-acceptance, toward clear direction and a more compelling personal purpose. It explains how our leadership stories can be incredibly rich if we take the time to use them in service of our own development. Importantly, the practices you'll read about in these pages come from deep research tested through an active leadership development practice. All the material that I cover in these pages and each of the practices I recommend to transitioning leaders has been tested and refined through work with hundreds of executives from all types of organizations.

It's worth noting that while most of the transition literature deals with the tactics of managing role changes, *Leadership Transition* is for leaders who, for whatever reason, suddenly find themselves having to make sense of new worlds that defy easy sense-making. It is for leaders who are between one way of working and the next. These in-between movements usually take the form of *new roles, new leadership, evolving structures, changing cultures* and *shifting life circumstances*. Each type of transition comes with its own challenges.

New roles challenge our skills, old mindsets and even our sense of how well we are travelling along the path of our lives. Stepping into a new role means stepping out of what has worked before and examining how the new world around us operates and how we want to operate in it, especially if our new role requires fundamentally different approaches to leading – for example, if we are transitioning to leadership for the first time, or to leading an entire business or function, or to enterprise leadership. Deeper emotions often sit below the surface of these role changes. They show themselves in the form of persistent doubts, an inner voice that asks us: *Will I be good enough? Do I deserve this? Is this the move that finally shows how I've been making it all up as I go along?*

New leadership also challenge our old approaches, but often in more subtle and more difficult ways. Adjusting to a new line manager can test our deeper assumptions about fairness, about how we are recognized and appreciated, and about the extent to which we've earned the right to be left alone, even by a new boss. A common reaction for senior leaders who are experiencing a change in their own leadership is to simultaneously *move toward* and *move against*: toward feeling the need to please this person to whom we've suddenly become vulnerable, and against in the sense of feeling some resentment that no matter how much we've achieved, there are always people we need to please.

Evolving structures come when the organization changes its form. Clarity often suffers during these adjustments, especially when they start at the highest levels and trickle their way through the organization. We might hope that our familiarity with the old organization will help us work our way through structural change, but a false sense of familiarity works against us. The landmarks may look the same, but the terrain around us becomes strangely different. Two examples of structural change from my practice shed some light on their psychological consequences. In one case, a top-down restructuring left senior leadership agreeing in principle but deeply confused in practice. *Why were those people fired (subtext: I would've fired a whole different set of people)? Why do we compete for roles in the new structure when we've proved our value here over many years? When will we know how the restructuring affects the lower levels of the hierarchy, because people are asking questions and they have options.* In a second case, the executive committee of an organization wondered why their most senior leaders were so critical of the company in the latest engagement survey. After some exploration, we wondered if what they were really voicing was a sense that after a series of acquisitions, they didn't recognize their old organization anymore.

Somebody had reconstructed their home in small steps, without warning them, and suddenly they didn't recognize where they were.

Like evolving structures, **evolving cultures** can be a shock to the system or a gentle change in a strange direction. In my leadership story, culture change happened quickly when it became clear that our senior leadership was not going to hold their colleagues accountable. In a similar example, a client tells the story of a new CEO who brought in an entirely different set of expectations about how leaders were supposed to behave. "We used to value the hard, boring work of being honest with each other and getting difficult things done," he told me. "Now the people who get ahead are the ones who pretend to agree with things they know are wrong, and who put together slick Powerpoint presentations rather than doing the hard work." Also like evolving structures, important cultural shifts happen below the surface. We might not be ready for the threat of what's coming because so much around us still feels familiar.

I'll spend more time on **shifting life circumstances** when I cover depth psychology in Chapter 2, but for now I'll say that sometimes the most important changes to our sense of leadership happen because of transitions outside of work. Life's many passages can cause us to question why we are doing what we are doing. I work with a woman who is exploring what it would mean to become the next CEO of her organization. She notices how her aging parents and growing children are challenging old notions of how her leadership plays into the story she wants to make of her life. "I'm almost 50," she says. "What do I really want to do with the next ten years?" She means: "Do I really want to become the next CEO or am I following that path just because people think that I should?" As we will see, life's natural passages can be our most powerful transitional experiences. If we pay attention, they force us to reflect on who we are and how we've become that person. They also force us to think differently about who we want to become. If leadership is an important stage on which we act out an important part of our lives, transitions outside of our work force us to explore how the story of our leadership really contributes, or fails to contribute, to the good story of us.

QUESTIONS FROM THE SPACE IN BETWEEN

Each of these transitions take the leader into what anthropologists call liminal space. Liminal space is the space you are in after you leave behind who you were but before you've become who you will be. Anthropology notes how much care and attention is given to navigating natural transitions in tribal life – from childhood to adulthood, from single to married, from adult to venerated elder. It also notes how the liminal space between set stages in life are devoid of the usual rules that govern how we think about who we are. Our challenge in this space is to sort out the new rules of the game, as we see them, and also to sort out who we will be once we have left the old us behind.

In the months that followed my story-sharing with Ash, I heard more stories of being in between from leaders who struggled with their transitions. Their many narratives convinced me to shift my research away from a conventional look at leadership transitions toward what felt like a much more interesting and relevant exploration of the psychological mechanisms that come into play when leaders suddenly find themselves stepping into new worlds. As far as I could tell, the territory was largely untouched in the field of leadership development.

I wanted the research to answer three questions.

First, I wanted to understand if it was correct to think of leadership transitions the way an anthropologist might think about tribal passages, or a clinical psychologist might think about our movements through life's disruptive events. That is, that they are events that are important enough to require special attention and deliberate care, and too dangerous to ignore. Thanks to my personal experience and the stories I'd heard from other leaders who'd navigated their way through life-changing transitions, I wondered if leaders are often forced to work through the significant psychological confusion that can come from their transitions without guidance. I wondered if I was part of a small and unfortunate group of leaders who'd somehow found themselves in unusually painful circumstances, or if leaders frequently feel pushed to the edge of their psychological stability. Some deeper questions emerged. If the feeling of being *in between* is a common experience for leaders, how common is it? And if these leadership experiences *are* common, why were the psychological dimensions of leading in between ignored in the popular work on leadership transitions?

Second, I wanted to understand what we know about how we manage ourselves successfully through such transitions. I wasn't interested in what conventional leadership development had to say about leadership transitions. I'd read all that I could get my hands on from the popular literature and understood how it focused on the tactics of the transitions rather than on the possibility of deeper destabilization. Instead, I wanted to know what anthropology might say about how we navigate transitions, and what our wisdom traditions might tell us, and what different schools of psychology might have observed. I wondered how all of these sources of knowledge might contribute to the story of how we navigate our way through life's storms and come out of them not just alive, but a better version of ourselves.

Finally, I wanted to know how whatever wisdom I could distill from all of these many sources could be translated into the realm of leadership. Are there any ways we can help leaders emerge from their experiences whole? Was there anything about clinical work with people in between that might help us understand how to work with leaders who find themselves at the edge of their capability, comfort or psychological stability? And if we do know something about helping destabilized people rediscover their balance, how can this knowledge help leaders whose limits are being tested through their leadership work?

In the years of research and in the practice that grew from it, I've worked with hundreds of leaders who've experienced what it means to lead at the edge. These leaders come from all different industries, work in all corners of the world, and operate at many different hierarchical levels. You'll meet some of them in the chapters ahead: B, the senior leader whose organization shifted under his feet despite his best efforts to keep it human, and who found that he had bent himself so out of shape to operate in it that he didn't recognize himself any more ("He was possessed," his wife told me, unaware that 'not being myself' is a common theme in clinical trauma work). O, the mountain guide whose years of service and hard work brought him to the presidency of one of the world's oldest and most venerated mountain guide's association, who discovered that moving from peer to presidency in such an organization can test the quality of even the oldest friendships. And L, the wise and smiling leader in a global financial services organization who gave up his hopes of reaching the top of the hierarchy once he saw that earning his way up to those levels seemed to require him to sacrifice important parts of who he wanted to be.

These leaders are typical of the people we support. Not all of them experience the same dramatic sense of destabilization, but all of them have had to navigate their way through difficult leadership storms. All of them have benefited from understanding how our minds tend to work when we are close to the edge, balancing between safe territory and the territory of dragons. Exploring the shift from one to the other led me to explore how a selection of clinical practices approach the psychological mechanisms at play during life's significant transitions. The work that follows brings the principles of the practice to you.

OUR ROAD AHEAD

There are good answers to my three questions.

Leaders *do* often feel at the edge of their competence, their self-understanding, their ability to cope and maintain a healthy sense of who they are and what is most meaningful to them. Not every transition pushes us to our edge, but almost all leaders, at some time or another, step into transitions that test our old assumptions. Almost all leaders are sometimes pushed beyond their capabilities.

Thanks in part to important recent clinical research into post-trauma growth, we understand how to emerge from even the most destabilizing experiences with a clearer sense of what is meaningful to us, a stronger understanding of who we are, and a deeper focus on the relationships and activities that help us grow. Our transitions, including our most difficult leadership transitions, turn out to be important laboratories for our own growth.

This book guides you through the challenges of your leadership transition so that you grow from the experience. I've structured the sharing into two parts.

Part One, *Treasure in Transition*, explains how our minds work when we step into the unknown.

Chapter 1, *Chaos, Creativity and Corruption*, frames leadership as a journey that takes place in between the forces of chaos and the forces of order. It describes the benefits of each and the dangers of too much of either, in the context of life and leadership. It leads us through the kinds of behaviours that indicate that we're in between. In the chapter I explain the importance of distinguishing between voluntary and involuntary challenge when it comes to our leadership and our personal growth.

In Chapter 2, *Poking the Elephant*, I turn to the wisdom we can take from different clinical schools of psychology about what it means to be in between. I begin to summarize the core observations of the five different schools of psychology that played an important role in my research: *existential psychology, evolutionary psychology, depth psychology, narrative psychology* and the *psychology of post-trauma growth*. Each school has its own point of view about what takes us to our edge, and each has unique contributions to the journey of turning our in-between experiences into profound personal growth.

Chapter 2 includes a dive into the technical details of how our minds work when we are at our limits.

I've included these details here because I think they matter, not least because they give insight into our unconscious psychological reflexes when our mental worlds are stressed. They also provide the research base for the work, which might be reassuring to any readers who are wondering if this is just another leadership book based on interesting but unsubstantiated ideas. All the ideas that I share here come from clinical practice and, importantly, all have been refined and integrated successfully into work with transitioning leaders at all levels and in many different organizations.

Chapter 3, *Wise Narratives*, explains the importance of our inner narratives, especially when it comes to navigating life's transitions. We are narrative-making organisms, and the quality of our inner narrative has an enormous influence over how we see the world around us and how we see and understand ourselves. Clinical practice describes the heart of the growth-through-transition process as one that leads to a wiser narrative. In Chapter 3, I'll describe what we mean by wise (and unwise) narratives, the importance of maintaining authorship over your life and your leadership, and the most important contributors to the creation of our wise narratives.

Part Two describes ***The Leader's Compass***, a way of organizing our most important inner narratives so that we stay focused and resilient when we step into transitional territory. The Leader's Compass structures our four most important inner narratives as if they were four points of an inner compass, with each compass point describing an important part of who we are and what is important to us. If the world of leadership sometimes brings us storms, the Leader's Compass keeps us aimed in the right direction and feeling grounded no matter how violent the winds and waters around us might be.

A well-explored and wise Leader's Compass is at the heart of how we turn even our most challenging transitions into profound personal growth.

Chapter 4, *Orientation*, is our North point. Orientation is the wise narrative we construct about where we are headed in our life and in our leadership and why we are headed that way. Creating the narrative of our Orientation forces us to explore what is most meaningful for us and why. It describes the difference we want to make, the impact we want to have, the legacy we want to leave. In Chapter 4, I explain how a clear, well-explored Orientation guides us through difficult choices, keeps us moving ahead when the currents around us may be trying to push us in different directions, and gives deeper meaning to our work.

Chapter 5 explores our *Roots*, our South point of the Leader's Compass. The wise narrative of our Roots is formed through an exploration of the values that sit highest in our value hierarchy and the beliefs that form the core of our 'operating system' in life. In Chapter 5, we explore how we can best understand our values and beliefs, as well as the aspects of our lives for which we are most grateful.

Chapter 6 explains the East point of our Leader's Compass, our *Relationships*. Here we set aside the usual stakeholder-mapping that is often a tactical part of navigating leadership transitions. Instead, we focus on the three relationships that matter most when you step into transitional territory: your relationship with your secure bases, your relationship with the organization that currently employs you, and your relationship with yourself.

Chapter 7 explores our *Resources*, the West point of our Leader's Compass. We explore three different resources that enable us to make a difference and that keep us stable in the face of transitional storms: our skills, our character strengths, and the activities that sustain and renew us.

In each of the chapters I describe what I mean by each compass point, what contributes to a wise narrative at each compass point, and also how to avoid common traps that can prevent us from creating wise narratives. The process of crafting our wise narratives is a creative and experimental process. There are no *exactly right* answers in the world of wise narratives, but there are useful answers and answers that are less helpful.

STEPPING INTO TRANSITIONAL TERRITORY

I have one final story to tell before we jump into the content. I tell the story as a guide to how to approach the material in this book. One of my early readings about the clinical process of personal transformation describes it as a four-stage discipline. The four stages are *Confession*, *Elucidation*, *Education* and *Transformation*.[1]

Confession is the sharing of a thought, a feeling, a belief or a behaviour that needs exploration because it's holding us back. In clinical terms, confession is the act of sharing the part of your story that you want to explore with the person or people who will join you in the exploration. *Elucidation* is the process of digging into the story to understand what might really be going on in you, beyond the obvious and below the surface. *Education* is exploring what can be done with what you've discovered through your digging beyond and below, based on all we know about how our minds have been shaped and how they tend to operate. And *Transformation* is what happens when you do the hard work of challenging and changing the beliefs, assumptions, convictions and mental habits that no longer serve you.

Conventional leadership development tends to start and finish with *confession*. There are good reasons for this self-imposed limitation. Confession feels good. There is a euphoria that accompanies the act of telling our stories and having them understood, appreciated and explored by others. There is a joy to lifting the loneliness of our untold stories. But, for good or for bad, development only happens when we leave the temporary euphoria of confession and get to the harder work of the next three stages. This movement forward requires effort, discipline, detachment and, above all, a compassionate curiosity that enables us to be honest with ourselves. This is challenging work – work that is unlikely to result in five-out-of-five scores in the conventional forms we use to evaluate leadership development programs. It walks us into uncomfortable territory. The discomfort of it means that it is exactly the right territory for exploration.

Leadership Transition is an invitation to come into that territory. In the pages that follow, I'll share openly and honestly what I've found helps leaders who want to use their transitions to understand themselves better and to guide themselves more wisely. I'll do my best to make what I've learned in the research and through my practice useful for you. My experience is that the practice works better when we understand the theory behind it, so I'll cover enough of the theory to make sure that you know where it comes from and why it matters. But as much as I appreciate the theory, I'll try not to get so bogged down in it that it feels like the point of the work. The point of the work is you and your growth, not the defense of the theory behind it. You are the case study.

I won't be promising you the *five things you need to do as a leader to live happily ever after*, or the *seven practices that will take you to leadership excellence*. I will be sharing with you some practices, approaches and ways of thinking about the task of leadership, and ways of thinking about yourself as a leader that should help you navigate through leadership's inevitable storms and come out the other side a wiser version of yourself. The work ahead may take some effort, some reflection, some frustration, some exploration. The answers aren't always easy or evident. It may take some uncomfortable digging to uncover your treasures, but the wisdom in them makes the work worth the effort.

TREASURE IN TRANSITION

CHAPTER I

CHAOS, CREATIVITY AND CORRUPTION

FRAMING THE TRANSITIONAL EXPERIENCE

The creation of something new is not accomplished by the intellect but by the play instinct acting from inner necessity. The creative mind plays with the objects it loves.

- CARL JUNG,
PSYCHOLOGICAL TYPES

LEADERSHIP, ORDER AND CHAOS

We need primary frames to make sense of our worlds. Primary frames are the main mental models we use to navigate our lives. We create primary frames to organize our thinking about how the world works and about how we should work in it. Our primary frames are the inner maps that tell us how to manage our relationships, how to lead our lives, even how to be a leader.[2]

We'll start our leadership transitions work with a primary frame that helps us understand what we are actually doing when we step out of one leadership role and into another. Our frame is the frame of *order* and *chaos*. A useful way to think about leadership, or about life for that matter, is as something that's lived in the tension between stability (*order*) and disruption (*chaos*). The experience of transition comes when we move out of the stability of order into the disruption of chaos.

The order end of our order-chaos polarity is *stability*, *predictability*, *clarity*, the *known* and the *expected*. In evolutionary terms, order is when your tribe has reliable sources of food, access to drinkable water, friendly neighbours, walls or weapons to keep the most dangerous predators at bay, and good health. Order is the alliance between humans and elves and dwarves in Middle Earth, the hierarchy of wise wizards in Harry Potter, or when the Avengers assemble.[3] In leadership, order is when good strategies are in place and working well, when people are behaving in ways that are consistent with the organization's best interests, and when our processes and structures are aligned, efficient and effective. Order is when we all understand where we're supposed to be going, and we all know what we are supposed to do to help us get there. We feel a sense of order when we know all the important people around us, we understand them, and we can safely guess how they will act. Order is when our leaders keep the promises they make, and when we can be confident that the organization will not prevent us from keeping the promises we make on its behalf. Organizations have all sorts of ordering mechanisms to keep chaos at bay. Strategies, plans, structures, processes, leadership principles, culture models, purpose statements, competence frameworks, our weekly management meeting, the monthly newsletter: these are all designed to bring some stability and predictability to an ever-changing and ever-threatening outside world. In my leadership story, a sense of order came from my deep knowledge of the organization, my many years of success in it, consistently positive performance reviews, established relationships, and a certain expertise in my field. Ash's sense of order would have come from her deep technical expertise, and a belief that a serious global organization would want her to do the work it hired her to do with unwavering commitment and professionalism.

At the other end of our order-chaos frame is chaos. Chaos is disruption, erratic change, the unknown and the unpredictable. We all live in chaos, since the world outside of us doesn't seem to be interested in our comfort and stability. We have to earn it. Chaos is all the things that change around us, even when we don't want them to change. Chaos is what is new and different. In evolutionary terms, chaos is the new pathogen, the entry of a threatening tribe on the borders of our territory, a diminishing food supply or the natural disaster that wipes out our village. In leadership, chaos is the new CEO bringing in unusual strategies and a fresh cast of senior leaders. Chaos is the new competitor entering our field or the new technology rending ours obsolete. Chaos is the latest restructuring, the newest acquisition and the forthcoming transformation initiative. Chaos is when you finally get that promotion and discover a few weeks into the role that the work is not at all what you expected it to be. It is when you're hired into a role and prevented from performing it properly by the very people who hired you (part of Ash's story). In our lives outside of work, chaos is the new relationship, the birth of a child, the passing of a loved one. It's an unexpected health issue or a broken relationship or moving to a new town or deciding to make a change in your career trajectory.

CHAOS, CREATIVITY AND CORRUPTION

In our lives and in our leadership, we rely on ordering mechanisms to help us navigate our way through life's chaos. Given how much chaos the world tends to throw at us and how much chaos the task of leadership asks us to confront, it's not surprising that we bring our instinct for ordering into organizational life.[4] Our ability to survive depends on our ability to re-establish order when chaos hits. The real challenge, in our lives and in our leadership, however, is to play in the creative space between order and chaos rather than to risk the corruption that comes when we are too ordered or too chaotic for too long.

Too much order means stagnation. It means the atrophying of the mental muscles that enable us to react constructively to the inevitable chaos we face in our lives. Stagnating order shows up in our work when the organization serves the preservation of the current more than it serves its own growth, and when outdated processes or limiting structures stay in place even when they prevent the company from performing as well as it could. Too much order is a culture that judges according to how things have always been done rather than encourages curiosity about how things could be done better. Too much order is when we preserve but don't create, when we protect rather than grow, and when we fear what could happen more than we aspire toward what might be better. It is beliefs that don't change even when we have overwhelming evidence that they are invalid beliefs. Too much order corrupts our ability to learn, grow, gain wisdom, pivot our sense of what is right or wrong, even change our sense of who we are and what is important to us.

The blessing of chaos is that it encourages us to grow. If we engage with it properly, chaos opens up territory for exploration and experimentation. Chaos is necessary for us to progress, develop, become even better companies, and better versions of ourselves as leaders. Chaos forces us to be creative. It tests who we are and what we believe and how we imagine success in our lives. Chaos keeps us awake and aware and ready to explore – in the words of Yvon Chouinard, founder of Patagonia, chaos keeps us "super alert, hungry, but not weak, and ready to hunt."[5] Chaos is good, until it overwhelms. Then it shuts down our ability to create and engages the part of our brain that wants to protect. Too much chaos, like too much order, comes with its own corruption. Too much chaos corrupts our ability to act with confidence, to be sure of ourselves, to relax and breathe, to feel safe. Too much chaos for too long keeps us in threat-response mode. It leads to confusion, burnout and psychological trauma.

If we value growth in our lives, our task is to use chaos as a territory for testing ourselves, for paying attention to the things in us that don't work, and for abandoning those things for better alternatives. If we value growth in our leadership, our task is to use the inevitable chaos that comes with our leadership as a laboratory for our psychological development.

This delicate balancing is at the heart of what it means to step into a leadership transition. Our role as leaders is not just to bring order. It is not just to build and protect. It is also to introduce chaos: to destroy and reconstruct. To bring in chaos effectively, to be confident and agile navigating ourselves and the people around us through chaos, we need to be capable of managing in that space of creative exploration at the edge of overwhelming chaos. We think of this as the work of flourishing in the creative tension between order and chaos, the space of healthy exploration and growth between the two polarities.

THREE OUTCOMES OF TRANSITION

What's at stake when we step into chaos? Take a minute to think of a time in your life when an event or experience profoundly changed you. We have all lived through these experiences. A family move, entering university, being truly independent for the first time, or the breakdown of a relationship, struggling through a new job, navigating yourself through a health crisis. Each of these occasions can challenge how we think about our lives and ourselves and can force us to create new ways. Sometimes this re-creation is easy. Sometimes it feels impossible. For the rest of this chapter, I'll dive into the fundamentals of transitional territory to set the stage for deeper exploration in the chapters to come.

First, it's useful to understand that the disruption of chaos typically leads to one of three outcomes. One outcome is bad. One is good. And one is even better.

A bad outcome of an edge experience is when we are significantly damaged because of the experience, and we are unable to repair ourselves. If you know anyone who has been broken because of a work experience, a health crisis, a physical or psychological trauma, and who is less functional than they once were because of it, you'll be familiar with what it means to be diminished by experience. In leadership, the corruption of being broken shows up in two ways. It shows up in the person who has lost their self-confidence. Ash had the sense of being broken when she and I met. So did I at the time. Broken is when we are so confused by an experience that we are unable to explore it and take anything useful or meaningful from it. Being broken is when the protective emotions that arise in the destructive experiences – the anger, the hate, the pessimism, the bitterness and the cynicism

– become the lens through which we see all of our experiences, even the ones that we would once have thought were positive. Being broken is the mental confusion that comes when a destructive event sets our reactive mechanisms on high alert, when we become hyper-aware of the possibility of danger around us, so much so that we see threats even where they don't exist. On a more subtle level, being broken is when we struggle to recreate a sense of who we are and of what is important to us.

For me, part of being broken was losing a sense of 'me.' This senselessness showed up in a strange way when I found myself having to tell the story of me to a group of strangers and came up empty. I was still working my way through painful negotiations over the terms of my departure from my old organization. I was in the early days of my research, and I was looking for new work after many years of employment in a place that had been small enough to feel intimate. It wasn't clear to me that I would find suitable work close to where we lived or that I would find new work that would enable us to maintain our lifestyle. It also wasn't clear to what a move would mean for my wife's young son, who lived with us but whose biological father is an essential member of our reconstructed family.

As it turns out, when you are active in the job market, the people you approach for work want to know who you are. I remember so often struggling with how to construct the narrative of me when asked the question. I couldn't rely on my old descriptors – *I have this senior role at this highly-regarded company, and I do these important things* – and no matter how hard I tried I couldn't come up with new descriptors that felt correct.

I took on some interim work with a leadership development boutique at the time. In that capacity I was asked to join a team of coaches supporting a program for partners at a professional services firm. At the opening of the program, we coaches were all asked to introduce ourselves so that the participants could choose who they wanted as their personal coach from among us. I remember trying to formulate a way of telling my story as I heard my fellow coaches tell theirs: *"I was a successful lawyer, now I do this," "I teach yoga and bring spiritual practice into my work," "I'm a psychotherapist and I can interpret your dreams during our breaks."* Their stories all seemed impressive and coherent. When my turn came, I struggled badly to tell the participants a short version of the story of me – so badly that when the time came for the participants to choose their coach for the program, the spaces under my name on the flipchart were the last to fill up. Although I managed my way through the program, I remember vividly the horrible hollow feeling of not knowing how to tell the story of me.

There are two better outcomes to transitional experiences than being broken. One of these outcomes is called resilience. Resilience has been a popular topic in the work of leadership development over the past decade, for good reason. As the task of leadership has become more complex and, therefore, more threatening, being resilient – technically, maintaining our form despite the forces trying to bend us out of shape – is an excellent outcome. Until the emergence of post-traumatic growth research in clinical practice, getting back to your previous level of functionality was the objective of clinical trauma work. Given how devastating disruptive experiences can be, maintaining functionality is an admirable result. Resilience, we know, comes from a well-researched list of mental and physical support mechanisms, including maintaining good relationships with close family members or friends, setting realistic goals, developing self-confidence, maintaining a hopeful outlook and taking care of one's physical health.[6] All of these sources of resilience have become popular topics in conventional leadership development.

Which leads us to the third and best outcome of transitional experiences. This is the outcome that drew the attention of clinical practitioners who were observing how different people reacted to traumatic experiences. It is the outcome that led to the emergence of a new field of trauma treatment that we now call post-traumatic growth. The field first emerged when clinical researchers observed that in some trauma cases, even when the trauma was extreme, certain victims were somehow able to use the experience as a catalyst for profound personal growth. We will get into the details of what exactly this means and how it seems to happen in Chapter 2, and we will borrow from clinical lessons in post-traumatic growth through the entire book. For now, it's enough to say that the initial clinical observations were both surprising and hopeful. Researchers found that, at least for some people, the lasting remarkable outcome of a deeply disruptive life experience was profound personal growth. Some people thought of their traumatic experience in such a positive light that the researchers coined the phrase 'sacred trauma' to describe them.[7] Sacred traumas were the experiences that victims would willingly repeat, given the chance to live their lives all over again, simply because of how much they value the personal reconstruction that would have been impossible without trauma's destruction. The work of my practice and the work of this book is to help transitioning leaders reach this outcome, no matter how challenging their leadership transition might be.

The chaos that she embodies is a shattering of rigid categories. If we enter into it, that chaos can resurrect us into a higher wisdom, rooted in the wisdom of the creative process. The chaos that we fear is the very thing that can free us.

- MARION WOODMAN,
DANCING IN THE FLAMES

VALUE IN THE SEISMIC EVENT

So, what do we know about leadership transition so far? We know that it's necessary to explore disorder if we want to keep ourselves, our teams and our companies growing. We know that a leadership transition is a step into the unknown, the new and the unexplored, the threatening and the creative. We know that stepping into a transitional experience means moving away from the comfort of order and immersing ourselves in the discomfort of chaos.

We know that immersing ourselves in transitional territory can lead to three outcomes. Growth and resilience are both good outcomes (although *resilience* can be the enemy of *growth* – more on that later). A bad outcome is to be broken by the experience. And since there are no guarantees of good outcomes from transitional experiences – think of all the organizations you know that have been crippled by failed mergers or transformation projects and the leaders you know who are still damaged by the stresses of their leadership – it's valid to ask why we leaders would take on the task of stepping into chaos voluntarily. Transitional experiences are risky experiences. Why would we ever step into them voluntarily?

There are two answers to the question. The first answer is that sometimes experiencing chaos is the only way to shake ourselves out of the seductive comfort of stagnating order. Psychologists have long known that we depend on our established worldviews to operate effectively in our worlds. They also know that a greater sense of security comes when some of these views are set in psychological stone. The benefit of our strongest core views – our *core narratives* or *core schemas* in the language of narrative psychology – is that they stabilize us in an unstable world.

The danger of inflexible worldviews, of course, is that they can prevent us from exploring new, more fertile or more mature psychological territory. This is the paradox of the inflexible worldview: it secures us and it limits at the same time. The more our worldviews secure us, the more important they are in our mental schemas of how the world works, the more difficult it is to let them go. In the words of existential psychologist Carlo Strenger, "Our need for a worldview that provides us with meaning is so overpowering that we will do almost anything to defend it."[8] In fact, early trauma researchers describe trauma as "very difficult circumstances that significantly challenge or invalidate important components of the person's assumptive world."[9] The more concrete and important a worldview is to us, the more it helps us make sense of the world, the more likely it is that we won't relinquish it voluntarily. We need an external event to do it for us.

Different schools of psychology have different language for experiences that shatter or violently reform our core narratives. Existential psychology sometimes refers to them as 'seismic events.' Jungian psychology notes how "catastrophe seems to be a necessary trigger for individuation."[10] Dan McAdams, one of the most prolific researchers in the field of narrative psychology, calls them 'nuclear episodes.' In his words, nuclear episodes ...

represent our subjective memories of particular events, in particular times and places, which have assumed especially prominent positions of who we were and, indeed, who we are. Nuclear episodes may include, but are not limited to, high points, low points, and turning points in our narrative account of the past.

Other kinds of nuclear episodes symbolize personal change or transformation. Many people describe dramatic turning points in which they came to a new understanding of self, or experienced a major change in their lives.[11]

The first answer to the question of why we take the risk of taking on a voluntary transition is that if we don't, we limit our ability to grow. The second answer is that there are ways to play with the amount of chaos you bring to your team or company or yourself so that it is a productive force rather than an overwhelming one. Working our way through in-between territory is risky, but there are ways to mitigate the risk. This is an important lesson from the research and from our practice. We don't always get to choose the events that shape us, but we can choose to build the psychological muscles that enable us to explore who we are with curiosity so that we are prepared to deal with any life-shaping experiences, whether or not they are voluntary or involuntary.

VOLUNTARY VERSUS INVOLUNTARY TRANSITION

The difference between voluntary and involuntary transitions is important because they tend to trigger different psychological mechanisms. When we decide to challenge our worldviews voluntarily, we are choosing to hold our beliefs, our assumptions, our worldviews and our sense of who we are up for exploration. We are implicitly treating all of these views as flexible. We can improve them in the face of the new evidence of our experiences. And we can explore all of these essential aspects of who we believe we are with curiosity and compassion, so that when involuntary change happens to us we have reliable and well-examined inner narratives to support us. Voluntary exploration to prepare for involuntary stress is the point of our practice, and the point of this book.

To understand why voluntary and involuntary stress are important to our work, it's useful to think about transitional experiences as experiences that take place in a space where the source of our stress intersects with the object of the stress. These are the two dimensions of transitional stress that trigger our psychological responses. If we take on our stress voluntarily, we are much more likely to engage in the work with positive, generative emotions. If our stress comes to us through no choice of our own, we are more likely to react to the stress with negative, protective emotion.

Likewise, we are more likely to be overwhelmed by events or experiences that challenge our core beliefs (our core schemas, in clinical terms). Our psychological defense mechanisms don't kick in with the same vigour to protect beliefs that are unimportant to our worldview.

Part of the dance of transitional work, then, is the dance of balancing between voluntary and involuntary stress and between exploring core and secondary narratives. If involuntary challenges are stressing the system, then we should minimize the voluntary stress we take on. If our core narratives are under attack, then we should minimize the extent to which we question our secondary narratives.

Leadership (or life) circumstances that we take on voluntarily and that don't require us to rethink important aspects of our worldview tend to be both comfortable and limited in their ability to help us grow. They don't cause us significant stress because our stakes in the developmental game are low. We work in this territory when we work with leaders who are in stable jobs that require no significant improvement in their leadership capabilities. To take some recent examples from our practice, leaders who would like to work on becoming more inspirational, or who want to be more effective public speakers, tend to think of these as comfortable challenges. They can be worked on methodically, over time, and under no significant pressure.

The challenge of low-growth developmental issues is maintaining the energy to do the work. This difficulty doesn't exist in the territory of involuntary challenges that shatter our most deeply held beliefs. This is, by clinical definition, the territory of trauma. Ash's transitional challenge arose when she was forced to decide whether or not she should do her job properly while fully believing that not doing so might put lives at risk. Choosing not to do what she believed the work required of her would have corrupted her deeply held personal beliefs about integrity, professionalism, ethics and morality. I faced a similar dilemma in my leadership story when

I was forced to choose between keeping my job or stepping aside so that powerful people who I felt were damaging the organization could do so without fear of my interference. Something important inside of me refused to step aside, perhaps because it understood that doing so would have compromised an essential part of who I wanted to be.

We work with these kinds of challenges in our practice as well. They are the challenges of the senior leader struggling to lead effectively when 20 years of dedicated service mean he is suddenly 'old school' in the eyes of the new CEO's team. They are the challenges of the new executive committee member who wrestles with how to maintain values that are critical to her sense of who she is when the committee's operating style feels unnecessarily diminishing. They are the challenges of the new CEO who has effectively led his sprawling global family-owned organization through the difficulties of COVID-19 only to find that the family member who chairs the board wants to conduct many of the CEO's activities himself. These are all transitional experiences that force the leader to examine their value systems and make difficult choices.

SUMMARY

Like many of life's important transitions, leadership transitions are a step into the unknown. They represent the same fundamental challenges to our ability to create and reorder ourselves in the face of chaos. They trigger the same psychological responses that chaos has triggered in us through our evolution. The creative tension between stagnating order and overwhelming chaos gives us an opportunity to grow.

When our transition is voluntary, or when it doesn't attack deeply held beliefs, it is unlikely to overwhelm our coping abilities. The more our transition feels involuntary or challenges important parts of our core narratives about how the world works, the more likely we are to feel fundamentally destabilized by the experience. For our leadership transitions to remain in the creative area of growth, we must understand the extent to which our transition represents a voluntary step into chaos or an involuntary one. We must also understand whether or not the transition is likely to challenge essential beliefs.

In the next chapter I'll describe how our brains tend to operate when we step into the territory of chaos. Before we go there, take a few minutes to write down your answers to the following three questions. Try to answer in complete sentences rather than bullet points. Answer as if we are having a casual conversation over a coffee, with no one else listening in.

1. Think of a transition in your life or in your work that was significant but not difficult. Although the transition marked the end of an important chapter in your life and the beginning of another one, you somehow managed the passage from one chapter to the next without much stress or anxiety. What was the transition, and what about it or about you made it relatively easy?

2. Now think of a transition that was also significant, but this time you struggled. What was this transition, and what about it or about you made it difficult?

3. In what ways did the first (easy) transition change you? What did you learn from it? In what ways did the second (difficult) transition change you? What did you learn from it?

CHAPTER 2

POKING THE ELEPHANT

HOW OUR MINDS WORK WHEN WE ARE IN TRANSITIONAL SPACE

The elephant, in contrast, is everything else. The elephant includes the gut feelings, visceral reactions, emotions and intuitions that comprise much of the automatic system. The elephant and the rider each have their own intelligence, and when they work together well they enable the unique brilliance of human beings.

- JONATHAN HAIDT,
THE HAPPINESS HYPOTHESIS

The moral psychologist Jonathan Haidt uses the metaphor of the elephant and the rider to illustrate the dynamic between our unconscious and conscious minds. The rider, he writes, thinks it's in charge, but it's the elephant who often decides where they both go. In Haidt's illustration, our rider is the holder of our rational thinking processes, the part of our brains that analyses what's going on around us, that makes calculations, draws conclusions and decides on logical courses of action. Our elephant, on the other hand, is our unconscious mind, the holder of our instincts and urges, our intuitions, the coping mechanisms we developed at such a young age that we didn't realize we were developing them, and the parts of ourselves that we hide because we don't like them or because we think the people around us won't like them either.[12] Haidt shares that even when the rider thinks it's made important choices, it is often just rationalizing the elephant's choices. Our conscious mind is often not much more than a way of processing the decisions we've already made for reasons we can't consciously explain.

In the next two chapters I'll explore how the unconscious mind works when we enter into transitional territory. I included this exploration in my research because I knew two things about my own transitional experience: I knew that I often didn't understand my own behaviour, and I knew that different schools of psychology have different ways of looking at how we function when we are under stress. Exploring how the mind works in transitional space would help me understand why so often I didn't recognize myself during my time in between. It would help me understand my elephant.

Five schools of psychology helped me the most. These were:

1. *Evolutionary psychology,* which sees the mind and its operating mechanisms as the product of tens of thousands of years of adaptation to survive as a social species in a harsh and unforgiving environment. According to evolutionary psychology, our oldest evolutionary instincts are alive and well and ready to express themselves, even in our modern environment.

2. *Existential psychology,* which describes our psychological lives as a struggle to find personal meaning that is profound enough to justify our inevitable challenges and to guide us through the overwhelming uncertainty around us.

3. *Analytical psychology,* which explores the process of becoming a version of ourselves that lives our life authentically, honestly, with deep self-understanding and, especially in the second half of life, free from the limiting sacrifices we've made to fit in. Analytical psychology uses the concept of individuation to explain how our riders and our elephants can understand themselves and each other better in the service of the person you truly want to be.

4. The *psychology of post-traumatic growth,* which describes how our most challenging transitional experiences give us important opportunities to examine and reconstruct the worldviews and self-views that so often guide our behaviour and so often sit outside of our conscious awareness.

5. *Narrative psychology*, which explores the role our inner narratives have in shaping how we experience the world around us. Our imaginations create stories out of our experiences to make them meaningful. If the language of our elephant is metaphor, story, image and symbol, narrative psychology is a deep exploration of how we can make sense of what our elephant is telling us.

I'll explore the first three of these five schools in this chapter. I'll dedicate the next chapter to post-traumatic growth and our narrative worlds, both of which are useful for understanding our elephants when they are badly wounded or under extreme stress – say, the stress of taking on a new leadership role. I separate these two fields out because they are new and because their wisdom is especially important for our work. Keep in mind that it's common for us to draw from all five of these schools (and others) in any given client engagement. This is normal, and one of the reasons I decided to cast a wide net in my research rather than to focus only on one type of clinical practice. All five of these clinical schools have important lessons to teach leaders at the edge, and none of them has a monopoly on the truth.

Finally, I'll use a story from the practice to show how each of the five schools of psychology would make sense of what is going on beneath the surface during a difficult leadership transition. It is a good example of how rich elephant territory can be when we are struggling to find our way through transitional work. I'll share the story with you as it was shared with me over a series of personal sessions with a client I'll call Matthew.[13] My work with Matthew started after he had moved away from the organization he describes in the story. The objective of our exploration was to make sense of his painful transitional experience after the fact so that he could navigate through future transitions with greater wisdom. Matthew had a successful career in the organization, but his story in it came to a difficult end because of a transition that he accepted even though he felt that the organization was shifting away from its values at the time. Matthew remembered a few warning signs along the way that he wished he'd paid more attention to. In our analogy, they were nudges from his elephant, warning him to be careful. The following story summarizes one of his elephant moments:

I remember so much about what it was like to try to navigate myself into the new role. I remember how I'd been feeling a little bored and maybe a little too comfortable when I was asked to take it on. I remember feeling proud of my track record in the company. I'd been there for well over ten years when the founder asked me to take on the new role. I remember how we'd suggested other restructuring possibilities to him when he asked us to take away important responsibilities from my boss, who was the managing director at the time. The founder refused all of them. Instead, he asked me to take on the role that we'd been trying to convince him to ask one of our colleagues to take. I remember being flattered that a leader of his stature would ask me to take on such an important task. And, also, being a little confused that he thought I could do it. There was a strange tension inside of me between the part of me that was eager and confident and wanted to take on a fresh challenge and another part of me that doubted and was a little bit afraid because it understood all the dangers that would come with accepting the new role. That part of me wondered if the move was really just a trap.

I also remember how the founder didn't include my boss in the restructuring discussions, even though the founder's restructuring idea would take some important responsibilities away from him.

It must have been a blow to his ego to have his boss ask a couple of people who reported to him to take over so much of his work. The founder didn't seem to care too much about how my boss might react to the change. If I'd been more myself in those days, I might've paid more attention to my boss's reaction. But I didn't appreciate him much. I kind of agreed with the founder when he criticized my boss's lack of leadership. So instead of thinking about how my boss might be threatened by the move, I focused on how it might be an opportunity for me — to advance, to be more important, maybe to have slightly higher status in the organization, although I wasn't and wouldn't be part of the elite partner group.

Anyway, we were doing well, I was comfortable in my seat on the Executive Committee, and was feeling pretty satisfied with myself when the founder proposed a restructuring that had me taking over an important part of the organization. I didn't say yes right away, even though part of me wanted to be a good soldier and do what I was told. I held out at first because I wanted to know more. I'm not sure what I wanted to know more of. Something in me sensed the danger ahead, I guess. Something in me told me to be very, very careful.

I was straddling both sides of the decision when the founder asked me to join him for dinner at a posh restaurant near our offices to discuss his proposal. He invited my boss as well. At least I think he did. I seem to remember that he was with us, although I don't think he said much. It's the nicest restaurant in the area. It's the place where the rich and famous go when they want to catch up or do business. All white linen and crystal glasses and hushed conversations under dim light. If the founder was impressed by the place, he didn't show it. I suppose he must've eaten at countless posh restaurants. Maybe they all blend together for him. But I was impressed. I was impressed to be at such a place. I was impressed to be having a conversation with him. I was impressed that he asked me to dinner so that he could convince me to take on the new role that he imagined for me.

The dinner conversation was mainly one way. My boss was conspicuously quiet through most of the evening. His boss, the founder, did most of the talking. All his talking was in the service of convincing me to take on the new responsibilities implied by the restructuring. Since he was a local captain of business, I imagined that he had deep layers of experience and wisdom. When he talked, I paid attention. When he explained yet again why he thought the restructuring was a good idea, I listened carefully. When he spoke favourably about my work, I felt proud in a strange "I'm a good boy" kind of way. I remember noticing the feeling and liking and hating it at the same time.

But I knew there was danger ahead. When the founder asked me to take over the team that had been reporting to my boss, he was asking me to take on a highly political group of people whose power came from the deep connections they sometimes created with our organization's privileged class. He was also asking me to take seriously the rules and regulations that were designed to prevent the same privileged class from competing against the organization that paid their salaries. Over my years working at the organization, these rules had proved to be essential to our health. Previous managing directors had fought hard to enforce them.

Over dinner, I noticed two voices in me competing for space.

One part of me wanted to listen and pay attention and be a good soldier and do whatever my senior leadership asked me to do. This part of me believed that the leaders above me knew what they were talking about, that they had far more expertise than I did when it came to issues of strategy and structure, that they were good and honest and trustworthy people. This part of me felt a little naïve, and maybe a little too eager to please.

Another part of me understood that the task I was being asked to take on was politically dangerous. I knew that others before me had failed to do what I was being asked to do. The unflinching support of these two senior leaders at the dinner table with me would be essential to my success. This part of me felt clear, mature, experienced and wise. Where the first part of me listened politely, asked a few questions and nodded in agreement, the second part of me wanted to share a little story with the founder and with my boss at our posh dinner table.

The story I wanted to share went something like this:

"You're asking me to take on a team that almost everyone has failed to lead successfully. You're asking me to confront the bad behaviour of more than a few members of our organization's privileged class.

"None of these important and powerful people will like it. Some of them will work hard to undermine me and the work you are asking me to do.

"There will come a point when they will force you to choose between me and them. You will choose them because they can hurt you and I can't.

"Unless we can sort out how to manage our way through this situation, we should forget about me or anyone else playing a part in the restructuring. We should keep things the way they are unless we agree on how to handle the inevitable and inevitably brutal response we'll receive from the few powerful people who won't like what you've asked me to do."

It would have taken me about 17 seconds to tell this story at our linen-and-crystal dinner table. I know because I said it out loud and timed it later. But a funny thing happened in that small moment. I didn't tell the story. I kept it inside of me. The first part of me won the battle for speaking rights on my inner stage. I nodded politely and told myself to trust the good intentions and the wisdom of my leaders. I took the job, and everything I predicted would happen did. I got fired for doing what I was asked to do.

Before I turn to an explanation of our first clinical school of psychology, think about an occasion in your life or in your leadership when two parts of you struggled over who gets to speak or make a decision or share a controversial point of view, and the part of you that you wish hadn't taken centre stage won the battle. This is probably a time when you withheld yourself, and when you wish you hadn't because withholding damaged you in some way. I'll use Matthew's story to explain the first school of clinical psychology in action. You can use your story to help make it meaningful for you.

THE CASE FOR EVOLUTION: PRIMITIVE INSTINCTS PLAYING OUT ON THE ORGANIZATIONAL STAGE

Our first insight comes from evolutionary psychology. Evolutionary psychology is founded on the observation that just as our bodies have evolved over millennia to help us survive and nurture the next generations in a harsh and demanding world, so too have our minds. We are physically constructed and psychologically programmed to survive, give birth to the next generation, and protect the next generation until they are able to fend for themselves. Over the many tens of thousands of years of our evolution, survival meant competing for scarce resources. Procreation meant securing a mate and organizing our families and tribes to maximize the likelihood that our children would survive long enough to have children of their own. Inside of us are all the instincts and urges, reactions and responses that are programmed into us, outside of our conscious awareness, by virtue of their value to our survival. Our elephants are holders of all that evolution has programmed into us because we wouldn't be here if it hadn't.

Researchers in evolutionary psychology note that our minds and bodies evolve slowly, with our incrementally changed genes competing for survival generation after generation after generation. They would also note that the pace of societal evolution over the past 200 years has been breathtakingly quick. In a real sense, our minds are now operating in a world that is strikingly different from the one for which they were designed. A great area of interest for clinical work in evolutionary psychology is the exploration of the ways in which our more primitive instincts play out on the modern stage. For leaders, of course, one of the main stages in which our evolutionary instincts and urges play out is the organizational stage.[14] The research shows two deeply embedded patterns of behaviour that are particularly interesting in the organizational setting.

The first pattern of behaviour comes in the form of a tension that is built into us. This tension is the desire to be personally powerful so that we can protect ourselves and those who are important to us and, at the same time, be able to connect and engage meaningfully with others because humans, out of necessity, are a social species. Evolutionary biologists refer to this tension as the tension between *agency* (personal power) and *communion* (relationship with others). We have a strong desire to be able to protect ourselves from harm, influence our surroundings so that they operate in our favour, and secure resources for ourselves and for our families. At the same time, we recognize that we limit our ability to survive individually if we don't make our collective survival a shared responsibility. My chances of making it on my own in a harsh, resource-scarce environment are low. They become much higher if I have a community around me that is also invested in my health and wellbeing.

Evolutionary psychologists argue that both agency and communion are critical to our ability to win at the evolutionary game. Our inner tension comes from the tendency for one of the two to dominate at the expense of the other. A second pattern of behaviour that is less a tension between behavioural patterns and more a range between them is what psychologists call *negative* and *positive* emotion. Evolution has programmed into us a set of emotions whose primary purpose is to protect us from harm. In some cases, these emotions seek to avoid the possibility of harm, while in other cases they react to the potential for harm once it presents itself. Think of fear, pessimism, cynicism and suspicion as threat-avoidance emotions, and anger, rage and subservience as members of the fight-flight-freeze-fawn set of threat-response emotions. All of these protective emotions tend to feel uncomfortable, for the obvious reason that if they felt good, we would go out of our way to put ourselves in danger.[15]

Our expansive emotions – what positive psychologists call positive emotions – are emotions that nudge us toward engagement, creativity and growth. These are the emotions that encourage us to connect socially, build community, explore new ways of doing things, experiment and learn. Imagine a socially cohesive tribe that shares a desire to explore new lands or experiment with fresh ways of generating plentiful food sources and you get a sense of the survival benefits of expansive emotions. We can include love, hope, optimism and joy in the expansive emotion set.

We all go into the task of leadership in organizational life with psychological programming that is designed primarily to help us survive in an environment that isn't designed for our comfort. When we take on the task of leadership, we take on the task of managing our ancient psychological mechanisms on a largely unfamiliar (in human psychology terms, and certainly in personal terms) stage. We also take on the task of understanding how all our inbuilt desires for all the attributes that have served us for thousands of years in tribal life – strength, status in the hierarchy, protective instincts and expansive urges – might be playing out in response to the cues we get when we lead in modern organizations. The task is complicated by our tendency to react to these cues as if we still lived in the environment of our evolution. We may *think* we react to threats in a measured, modern and sophisticated way, but the systems that kicked in when predators were approaching the tribe a few thousand years ago are the same elephant systems that kick in now when the latest transformation initiative threatens our place in the organization's dominance hierarchy.

We can see these systems at play in Matthew's story. Matthew's narrative begins when he's offered a more important role in the company hierarchy. Along with the role comes additional status. Status is good, since it is usually associated with greater security and greater access to resources (remember, Matthew's brain is operating according to the old evolutionarily beneficial assumption that more access to greater resources means more food, more shelter, greater attractiveness to the people who attract us, etc.).

The benefits of higher status would explain Matthew's initial positive instinct regarding the possibility of hierarchical advancement. In his case, however, advancement came with risk. Matthew recognizes almost immediately the threat of envious and powerful colleagues, and he understands clearly that in his organization, a privileged class of employee, something like partners in a professional services firm or doctors in a hospital, would always sit at the top of the status hierarchy. Matthew knows the organization well enough to understand that he would have limited power to navigate his way through the chaos he would be stepping into.

And so, as you'd expect from a mind designed for survival, Matthew wonders how to navigate the risk. The path he chose was to try to please the founder, a powerful leader whose support and protection would be crucial for his success. And he tries to nurture this relationship by relying on a strategy of subservience rather than by demonstrating personal power. For all sorts of reasons, Matthew's communal skills were much more developed than his skills at expressing personal agency. Hence his strange silence during their dinner conversation. The conversation was one in which Matthew was being set up to fail. He recognized that dynamic, and yet he still attempted to navigate his way to success with a strategy that had worked for him before. That is, by being agreeable.

It's a common strategy. We see it playing out in hierarchies all the time. It shows up when we withhold our opinion because someone higher in the hierarchy expresses an opposing one. Or when we do what we're told even when we believe it's the wrong thing to do. We may struggle with our own behaviour in these cases, but it's important to recognize that the behaviours that are playing out in us are deeply programmed, and that they have served us well over thousands of years.

While developing alliances with more powerful tribe members can work, in Matthew's case it failed badly. He took on the role he was asked to take. His work played out exactly as he had suspected it would. He was pitted against a small but more powerful group of players who organized themselves into a coalition. It was easier for the firm's senior leadership to sacrifice Matthew than to confront them. His attempts to build supportive relationships among this group were unsuccessful. No matter how calm and logical and rational he was at explaining what he and his team were doing, no matter how often he pointed to their excellent results, no matter how strong his convictions, he was fighting a losing game. The game came to a close when for the first time Matthew politely but openly confronted the founder and the managing director on the many ways in which they were setting him up to fail. Not long after, something like 12 years into his tenure at a small professional services organization that had become an important part of his life, Matthew was fired.

He was reassured when I told him that the protective emotions that showed up in him as the drama played out were consistent with what an evolutionary psychologist would expect from someone who feels under attack. All the confusion, anger, bitterness and hatred Matthew began to feel toward his organization and to the few from the privileged class who were working hard to get him out of the way were exactly what you'd expect from someone who believes that his life is in danger. You might think, *but was it really?* And an evolutionary psychologist's response might be, maybe not, but the psychological structures that were guiding his behaviour would be forgiven for not understanding the nuances of the situation. As far as Matthew's elephant was concerned, threats to his livelihood and his identity deserved a vigorous response, especially after his appeasement strategy failed.

For leaders operating on the edge, it's useful to keep in mind two fascinating observations from the clinical world that make sense from an evolutionary perspective. First, humiliation is a leading cause of violence inside and outside the workplace.[16] The more we feel humiliated, the more likely we are to respond violently. This is an important evolutionary instinct, since humiliation implies weakness, weakness implies vulnerability, and vulnerability implies danger. Second, a natural response from someone who has recently been bested by someone stronger is to immediately attempt to dominate someone who is weaker.[17] We are programmed to try to reestablish a sense of strength when we feel that we have been made to appear weak. It's worth remembering these two observations when we notice aggressive behaviour, bullying and mobbing in our organizations. Aggression in all its organizational forms initiates all sorts of interesting unconscious psychological responses. These responses were designed to help us cope with the harsh complexities of tribal life.

INSIGHT IN PRACTICE: LEADING WITH CURIOSITY BEFORE JUDGMENT

When we engage with executives who are undertaking leadership transitions or leading organizational transformations, it's always useful to explore what threats these changes might imply for their evolutionary instincts: for their hierarchical position, for their status, for their sense of influence, power and importance. It's also useful to pay close attention when protective (negative) emotions come into play. Anger, frustration, resentment and bitterness are normal responses to a perceived threat. Exploring the nature of this threat, whether it's real or not, and the extent to which it justifies the kind of response that evolution has programmed into us, helps our rider understand what the elephant might be experiencing. We humans are lucky, in a very real sense, that we have riders at all. We aren't prisoners of our evolutionary instincts. In the famous words of evolutionary biologist Richard Dawkins, we are unique as a species in that we can override our genetic programming. It's part of our programming to be able to consciously override our instincts. With exploration and effort, our riders can convince our elephants to change direction.[18]

The great lesson that evolutionary psychology gives to leaders is that for all our wonderful sophistication and intellect, we are driven by the same set of unconscious instincts that drove our tribal ancestors. We have the same deeply imbedded need for status, for access to resources, for security, for alliances. And we have the same strategies for gaining all of those things: the same desire to elevate ourselves, jockey for position against our competitors and win. Importantly, we also have the same ancient reactions when our competition gets brutal: the same instinct to fight (usually and thankfully with psychological rather than physical weapons), flee (by finding another job with a friendlier tribe), freeze (by doing the minimum required of us, or by remaining silent and, we hope, unnoticeable), and fawn (by seeking favour with the more powerful). Evolutionary psychology's lesson helps us frame our expectations of leadership. We may like to think that we all work together in relative harmony and with a modern rationality – and sometimes we do – but the behaviours we display in our leadership are the behaviours that were designed into us thousands of years ago for lives that are very different from the lives we lead now.

A second lesson that I took from evolutionary psychology is to lead with curiosity rather than with judgment when it comes to understanding human behaviour, including my own. I was raised in a cultural and religious background that sometimes tended toward judgment rather than curiosity. Anger, bitterness, jealousy, hatred and fear were all judged to be bad behaviours, sins in the common language of the religion. Evolutionary psychology reframed these behaviours for me. It taught me that just about every impulse we have has been useful in an evolutionary sense and all those so-called bad emotions can be useful. Understanding these emotions as an important part of my psychological programming helped me be curious about what to do with them once they showed up, knowing that they are imperfect impulses when it comes to navigating in a world that is strikingly different from the world for which we were designed. Being curious about how my instincts and impulses were playing out in me when I was under threat helped my conscious rider to engage with my unconscious elephant and to help guide it, at least partially.

THE CASE FOR MEANING: EXISTENTIAL ANXIETY AND THE NEED FOR SIGNIFICANCE

Existential psychology builds on evolutionary psychology's idea that our minds have adapted over millenia to help us cope with the challenges of a sometimes hostile world. But while evolutionary psychology frames our psychological mechanisms as those associated with survival, existential psychology frames them in terms of the unavoidable anxieties of human life. Evolutionary psychology says that our elephants are there to help us navigate our way in a confusing world. Existential psychology says that they bring with them some unavoidable anxieties about what it means to be human. Finding the right answers to questions about our human anxiety, or avoiding the questions altogether, is the territory of our elephant.

The existentialists describe four primary human anxieties: the anxiety of *death*, the anxiety of *freedom*, the anxiety of *isolation* and the anxiety of *meaninglessness*. According to existential psychology, we have choices to make when it comes to dealing with these anxieties. We can choose to ignore them as best we can (what existential psychology calls *forgetfulness of being*) or we can meet them head on, explore them, understand them and find honest ways to address them (what existential psychology calls *mindfulness of being*).[19]

Before I explain what all of this means for leaders in transition, I'll share more from Matthew's story. I'll once again use his material to translate the ideas of a clinical practice into the leadership domain. And I'll once again let Matthew tell his own story. As you read the words that follow, try to imagine how you would have managed yourself in his circumstances. Do you fight or do you appease?

Once I accepted the new role and got down to the business of making the founder's restructuring work, two things happened.

First, our results were good. Despite the difficult global economic circumstances, we strengthened our position in the market. We paid more attention to our clients. Our financial results improved. We got the usual praise and healthy bonuses because of the importance of our work. The founder actually gave me an especially healthy bonus, I think because he recognized how difficult it was to get the work done. An important part of me was satisfied with my work. I was happy for the recognition we received.

Second, the story I wanted to tell the founder over our dinner conversation – but didn't – came true. A few of the members of the organization's privileged class went outside of our rules and regulations to make more money. They did it in a way that made their behaviour impossible to ignore. It was my duty to call out this behaviour in the Executive Team, but I realized pretty quickly that doing my duty wasn't welcome. Most of the people on the Executive Team were friends with the people who were breaking the rules. Maybe some of them were breaking the rules themselves. First I was ignored. Then two of the offenders started a campaign of abuse and disinformation against me and my team.

The two offenders refused to talk directly to me. Neither the founder nor the managing director would risk engaging them in meaningful conversation, so my interactions with them were mediated through our organization's head of harassment. She was also a member of the privileged group, but she at least seemed concerned about how our culture was becoming poisoned. I remember one conversation I had with her as things were heating up and their efforts against me were gaining momentum. I sat across the table from her in her office. I was tired. I was worried. And I was very, very annoyed. We were meeting because she had had a conversation with the two partners who wanted me out of their way. She told me that I needed to prepare myself for a dirty fight.

"They won't stop until you step aside," she told me. "They have nothing to lose by trying to get you kicked out." It was true. They wouldn't be held accountable for behaviours that would've had them fired in most other organizations.

We talked for a little while about why my two adversaries were so eager to have me removed, but we both understood the subtext. With me out of the way and with one of them taking my place on the Executive Committee, they wouldn't have to worry as much about me calling for their accountability.

At the end of our conversation, the head of our harassment committee told me, "You have a choice. You can fight, or you can give up." There was a subtext here as well. We both knew that a member of staff taking on members of the privileged class was a battle with only one outcome.

I think she thought it would be wiser for me to give up. It didn't take me long to choose to fight, but it wasn't as straightforward a choice as I thought it would be. Despite all of my anger and all of the energy coming from what felt like a horrible betrayal, I was afraid. At first, I didn't understand why my fear was felt so deeply. I realized that I was afraid of what I might lose if I left an organization that had become so important to me. It sounds strange, doesn't it? After all, it's only a job, isn't it? But it was somehow much more than just a job.

OUR FOUR ANXIETIES

Here we get to the essentials of existential psychology and the ways we respond to its four essential fears or anxieties. Before we explore our coping mechanisms against the anxieties, I'll share more detail on the anxieties themselves.

By *anxiety of death*, the existential psychologists mean that of all the unknowns we face in our lives, the most fundamental and the most unavoidable is death. From a very early age – earlier than most of us recognize, according to the existentialists – we understand that our time here is limited. We also understand that while we may be taught some comforting beliefs of what comes after our life is over, these are, well, beliefs. We may *believe*, but we don't *know*. The anxiety of not knowing what comes after life is, in clinical terms, both significant and difficult to reconcile with our desire for a calm, peaceful, predictable and happy existence. It is difficult to enjoy the race when we don't know what happens once we reach the finish line.

By *anxiety of freedom*, we mean the psychological tension that comes with having to make choices, knowing that many of these choices have a weighty impact on how our lives will unfold (*this career* or *that one*; *this spouse* or *that one* ...). Having to choose also means having to relinquish possibilities. It means having to give up what might be down one road because we've chosen another one. We can't know where any of these monumental decisions may take us, and so we lack complete confidence that the outcomes of our choices will be good ones. Every choice is a deliberate step into the potentially threatening unknown. With every choice we are saying no to endless possibilities and saying yes to only one.

By *anxiety of isolation*, we mean the discomfort that comes from knowing our journey through life is our journey and our journey alone, no matter how many friends we have or how deep our intimate relationships might be. No one shares exactly our experiences or feels exactly our mysterious blend of anticipations and emotions. No one knows perfectly what it is like to be me, just as I don't really know what it is like to be someone else.[20] I may be privileged with the company of wise and wonderful people during my time here, but in the end my life is mine alone. No one else gets to experience the journey in quite the same way. In a very real sense, I am on my own, even when I want to believe that I am not.

Finally, by *anxiety of meaninglessness,* existential psychology means our unsettling suspicion that despite all our attempts to explain why we are here, the answer might well be *for no reason at all.* Before we fall back on religious justifications for our existence, let's remember the difference between *belief* and *knowledge.* What we believe is different than what we know (which is why science and faith are two largely different realms of exploration, and why existentialists are skeptical when we pretend that what we believe is what we know). The suspicion that there might not be a larger meaning to our existence given by an outside agent leaves us with the task of sorting out the meaning of our lives for ourselves. This self-determination of personal meaning is harder work than just accepting a purpose we've been taught. And, as it turns out, it is the essential act of dealing productively with all four anxieties.

Existential psychology encourages us to explore each of these anxieties for ourselves, and take on with energy and honesty the task of finding healthy answers to the questions behind them. I mentioned earlier that existential psychology differentiates between *forgetfulness of meaning* and *mindfulness of meaning* when it comes to our anxiety response strategies. Forgetfulness of meaning refers to our many mechanisms for trying to avoid our anxieties rather than to do the difficult work of confronting them head on. Organizational life, it turns out, can be a seductive source of forgetfulness.

COPING WITH OUR FEARS ON THE ORGANIZATIONAL STAGE

Four common coping mechanisms associated with each of the four anxieties are:

1. *feeling special*: mitigating our fear of death because our specialness means that life's usual rules and randomness might not apply to us;

2. *structure*: mitigating the anxiety of freedom by handing over our choices to an external authority;

3. *community*: mitigating our fear of isolation by surrounding ourselves with people who we feel value us;

4. *significance*: mitigating our fear of meaninglessness by attaching ourselves to a convenient source of purpose.

It's difficult to find good answers to the four anxieties. Each of these coping mechanisms can be approached honestly and with effort. Or we can try to avoid the hard work of finding good answers to them by accepting the easy comfort of shallow answers. This is where organizational life and leadership steps in. Being a leader gives us all sorts of ways to avoid the hard work of dealing with our anxieties honestly. For example:

Feeling special. Leadership is, by definition, the act of being set apart from followers. With leadership can come a sense that we have been chosen above others, or that we have special abilities that give us unusual influence. We celebrate when we are first appointed to leadership roles. We celebrate each step of the way up the leadership ladder, not just because of the financial rewards that tend to go along with such moves but because every step confirms our specialness. If we aren't careful, our leadership might convince us that we are so special that we don't need to worry about the usual randomness of life and its ending. I know in my leadership story the discomfort I felt taking on the new and risky role was counterbalanced in part by the fact of feeling special just because I was asked. I liked the feeling. While I didn't consciously imagine that my specialness would protect me from life's randomness, I imagine that some part of me hoped that it would.[21] Matthew felt the same seduction in his own leadership. He appreciated the sense of specialness that came with the responsibility of leadership. He felt a soothing sense that things would be OK, thanks in part to his special status.

Structure. Against the anxiety of choice, organizations provide comforting structure. To belong to an organization means to follow its rules and to integrate yourself into its systems and processes. It means understanding how the community of people who come together in the company have arranged themselves. It means learning its strategies and cultures and your role in supporting both. It also means following unspoken rules of engagement and ways of behaving and all the ordering mechanisms designed to keep the dogs of disorganization at bay. Organizations are ordering mechanisms. In return for the structure they give us, we who belong to organizations agree to operate according to their rules, abide by their processes, integrate ourselves into their systems – in short, relinquish many of our choices to the organization. This is especially true of leaders since we have typically benefited more than most from the organization's systems and we are often responsible for mastering and maintaining them. Matthew's understanding of the small organization in which he worked was such a source of personal comfort and stability for him that he sometimes wondered how well he could operate in a different system. This fear expressed itself in a common question leaders ask themselves, especially when they've served in one organization for a long time: *Is my success because of me, or is it because I have learned to operate well in this particular system?*

Community. Against the fear of isolation, organizations give us community. We might not always get the community we want, but we do get a community that shares physical and mental space with us, that is brought together for common purposes, and that nurtures itself over lunches and dinners and offsite meetings and countless coffees around the coffee machine. Our organizational lives provide us with people with whom we share hour upon hour of conversation and interaction, people with whom we can trade jokes or complaints, who listen to our stories and whose stories we listen to. They give us a sense of intimacy that diminishes our sense of aloneness. And if we are leaders, they can also give us a sense that our relationships matter, that the fellow leaders with whom we share the responsibility of steering our community are partners, bound together by a common cause.

As with an organization's structure, the community an organization provides can become especially seductive when we stay in it for a long time. The longer we are embedded in a community, the more that community shields us against our fear of isolation. This was especially true in Matthew's case. His many years at his organization meant that the line between collegiality and friendship blurred. He shared ski vacations with members of the organization's privileged class, socialized with them, saw their kids hang out together. Although there are benefits to this sense of closeness, the terrible vulnerability that comes with such strong community-building is that organizations don't exist to foster deep relationships. They exist for other purposes. Achieving these purposes takes precedence over the nurturing and preservation of whatever relationships might develop in the course of our work. Hence the anxiety we feel when work relationships are tested or broken because decisions favour strategic aims over human ones, a well-documented source of trauma, in the clinical sense, for more than a few leaders.[22]

Significance. Finally, we get to meaning, existential psychology's primary focus. According to existential psychology, we all have a deep desire for meaningful lives. Meaning gives us a justification for our struggles, for our effort, for the time we spend on this earth. Without meaning, we are aimless. Meaning, in existential terms, is the most powerful ordering mechanism we have against life's inevitable chaos. According to existential psychology, our most important life's work is to search for and find what is most essentially meaningful for us, at every stage of our lives.

The territory of meaning, however, is difficult territory to explore. How do I differentiate between what's really meaningful for me and what's presented to me as meaningful in whatever culture I belong to? How do I follow the shifts in what's meaningful for me as I pass from childhood to adolescence to adulthood to middle age and old age? How can I make my explorations of meaning useful when they are likely to uncover intuitions and urges rather than high-definition explanations?

Our organizational lives give us easy answers to these challenging questions. What's meaningful is the job you have, the key performance indicators you're expected to reach, the culture you're supposed to build and the organizational purpose you're supposed to strive toward. There's meaning to be found in that next step up the organizational hierarchy, or the success of the new business you've been asked to run, or the strengthening of the function you're now leading. Meaning is good results and advancement and helping the organization achieve its goals. These definitions of meaning are seductive – at least, they were for me and are for many of the leaders with whom we work. But unless the answers to our questions about what is most meaningful for us are explored deeply, they tend to be too shallow to keep our existential anxiety at bay indefinitely.

INSIGHT IN PRACTICE

All of these anxieties and coping mechanisms explain why we are often tempted to withhold ourselves in risky leadership situations. They explain why Matthew was so hesitant to take on a small group of his organization's powerful people, even though he felt his integrity demanded it. Confronting them came with the very real risk of jeopardizing a whole host of comfortable associations that came with his leadership: his sense of being special by virtue of his senior role, the ordering structure the organization gave to him, the community of friends he thought it brought him, and the belief it helped him to sustain that he was doing something intrinsically valuable through his work. All of these were shallow but comfortable answers to existential psychology's deepest questions. He protected these answers vigorously because of the comfort they brought to him.[23] It was easier, at least for a while, to protect them than to risk their destruction.

The great lesson that existential psychology gives leaders is that while we may believe that our work is everything it appears to be on the surface, much deeper psychological mechanisms are at play inside of us when we go about our leadership work. Our leadership roles give us much more than a steady paycheck and good bonuses. They give us comforting answers to uncomfortable questions. The organizational stage is a leader's primary stage for experience and exploration. For many leaders, it may sometimes feel like our most important stage. And while we may believe that our work on that stage is defined by the usual work of leadership – setting our strategies, designing our organizations, encouraging our teams – it is also a stage on which we live out the drama of our deepest fears and search for answers to our most profound questions. When leaders step into transitional space, it's worth asking which of our four anxieties might come into play. More importantly, it is worth using the transitional space to test the quality of our answers to life's four main anxieties.

THE CASE FOR BECOMING YOURSELF: THE LONG JOURNEY OF INDIVIDUATION

If existential psychology explains why Matthew was so hesitant to step into his leadership battle, analytical psychology explains why he decided to fight.

Existential psychology encourages us to find good answers to some profound questions about our lives. Analytical psychology – also called depth psychology – focuses on how we are to understand ourselves as we progress through our lives. It encourages us to do the hard work of exploring our elephants, even though we might not like a lot of what we find. This is where analytical psychology differs from evolutionary and existential psychology. Evolutionary psychology says that our elephants are products of evolution. Existential psychology says that they are holders of our human vulnerability. Analytical psychology says that our elephants are both of those things, but that they also hold the unconscious outcomes of deeper and more mysterious psychological struggles that come into play when we try to live authentic lives within the constraints of civilized society.

Like evolutionary psychology and existential psychology, I'll tell the story of analytical psychology in terms of the two ways in which it is most useful in our leadership work. First, I'll look at how analytical psychology frames the two main stages of our lives. Then I'll describe what the second stage – the stage analytical psychologists call *individuation* – can tell us about how to make sense of our lives and our leadership.

A LIFE IN TWO HALVES

A fundamental question of analytical psychology is, *"Whose life am I living?"* In analytical psychology, the answer to the question often depends on whether you are in the first half or the second half of your life.

We tend to dedicate the first half of our lives to the task of understanding how the worlds around us function and managing ourselves so that we reach some level of success in the context they provide. The first half of life is for identifying our talents and strengthening them, for choosing our careers, for starting families, for achieving conventional success. It is also for making sure that we get along, that we are acceptable, that whatever tribe we're part of will take care of us. And, finally, if we work at it, the first half of life is for developing a healthy ego. In analytical psychology, healthy ego refers to a well-functioning conscious mind and a strong sense of identity. Think of a healthy ego as a rider (remembering our rider and elephant metaphor) who is skilled at exploring and organizing their thoughts, feelings, senses, intuitions and memories. So, in many important ways, the answer to the question *"Whose life am I living?"* in the first half of life is *"the life I believe I need to succeed in my world."*

Once all of that is achieved – once we've managed our way through the first half of our lives to achieve some sense of success and security – we get to the second half of our lives. If the first half of life is for establishing ourselves and forming a healthy ego, the second half of life is for answering the question: *"Now that all that is done, who am I really?"*

Analytical psychology calls the process of finding a good answer to the question *"Who am I really?"* individuation. Individuation asks us to explore all the compromises we have made to fit in with our family, our tribe, even our work community, on our way to conventional success. It asks us to explore what essential parts of ourselves we may have suppressed or denied so that we are acceptable to the powerful people around us. It encourages us to look at the aspects of ourselves that scare or disturb us so much that they usually evade our conscious thought. Analytical psychology refers to all these repressed or denied beliefs, values, ideas, desires, wounds, weaknesses and instincts as our *shadow*. Understanding our shadow by bringing it into the light of conscious thought is the point of the analytical process. Our shadows sit in the territory of the elephant, whose behaviour expresses all of these denied parts of ourselves. The more we deny ourselves and the longer we deny it, the more likely it is that the elephant will behave in ways we don't like, don't understand and are helpless to control.

At the heart of individuation is understanding, making peace with and learning from our elephant. As it turns out, though, the elephant isn't easy to understand. Our rational, conscious rider-mind and our irrational, unconscious elephant-mind operate in different realms and speak in different languages. For the rider to truly understand the elephant, she must seek to also understand the realm in which the elephant operates and communicate with it in the language it speaks. That language is the language of image, symbol, metaphor, myth and imagination.

THE TASK OF BECOMING YOU

Analytical psychology has at least three important messages for transitioning leaders.

First, it is highly likely that on our path to leadership we've made unconscious choices that set aside important aspects of who we are. It is a common theme in our work, when we engage in conversations with leaders about where they've come from, that we hear about passions, dreams, interests and even important wounds that have been buried under the busyness of their work. Sometimes these essential elements seem to be insignificant and small and may take the form of a sport or art or practice that once captured their imagination but somehow got lost under new preoccupations. Sometimes they feel more monumental – a career choice that was expedient but not true to their deeper interests, or the passing of a loved source of encouragement and security at a young age – but are just as ignored. According to analytical psychology, we can only keep these essential elements of ourselves buried for so long. Our elephants have limited patience for staying passive under their weight. Sooner or later, they will express themselves. They are more likely to express themselves usefully if we do them the favour of trying to understand them. The more we keep them buried in the dark, the more damage they do to us. It is only by bringing them to light that we let them express themselves fully and helpfully.

Second, it is unlikely we've developed the necessary skills to work with our elephants in their realm, on their terms, using their language. Conventional leadership development favours the rider. In leadership we busy ourselves with strategies and structures and processes, on the standard measurement mechanisms, on the numbers that tell us about our financial performance.

We might have wandered in the realm of the elephant in a college mythology course or written in its language in our creative writing class in high school. We may step briefly into its territory when we watch a movie or read a book. But, for the most part, we've had to turn away from that realm when we are at work because organizations like to believe that the rider runs the show. So, when it finally comes time to attend to our elephant, we don't know how.

Third, our elephants tend to raise their voices during important life transitions, including career transitions. When a dramatic change in our career, our family lives or our living circumstances shakes up our riders, our elephants spot an opportunity to get themselves noticed. Then they speak up. Sometimes they speak up loudly. They speak up in ways that our riders don't recognize or understand. This explains why so much of our developmental work is with executives preparing for significant career transitions, including men and women who are stepping into the CEO role.[24] The importance of the rider during such moves explains why virtually all leadership development aimed at executives-in-transition is designed for the rider. But the elephant, sensing that an old constraining world is about to be left behind, will do its best to get noticed so that the next world is one that allows it to express itself more fully.

Here we come to an important observation in our work: many of the leaders we support are taking on their most challenging leadership transitions just as they are moving into the second half of their lives. Analytical psychology's belief that the elephant gets uncomfortably restless as we enter the second half of our lives coincides with the organizational reality that we leaders often step into our most challenging leadership roles at the same time. We're then faced with two strong currents swirling together: the outer current of taking on a role that might represent our first time leading in highly chaotic territory where loneliness and a sense of being overwhelmed are common, and the inner current of the deepest and most essential parts of ourselves insisting loudly and maybe for first time to be heard, respected and expressed.

INSIGHT IN PRACTICE

Our insight from evolutionary psychology tells us that our elephant contains all the drives and energies that helped us survive over tens of thousands of years. Our insight from existential psychology says that it also contains the fundamental deep fears that come with human vulnerability. Our third insight sees the elephant as the holder of all that is deep and mysterious and unexpressed in us and tells us that understanding our elephant in all its depth and mystery is essential to becoming who we are.

Analytical psychology might look at Matthew's leadership transition as the normal process someone goes through when they take on a difficult leadership role just as they're entering the second half of their life. The challenges of their new work might present them with all sorts of ways in which they could compromise themselves, their values, their sense of who they want to be, just as their unconscious is screaming at them to stop with all the corrupting compromises that bring them further away from the person they want to become. This is how Matthew came to understand his journey. He could have continued with his strategy of acquiescence. He could have agreed to step aside. He could have accepted being the scapegoat for the organization's creeping corruption. It would have been easy to accept that compromise. But he didn't. Something in him demanded to be heard. Matthew's elephant might not have expressed himself gracefully at the time – they usually don't when we haven't taken the time to understand them – but he was clear that the path of compromise he was being asked to take was far more dangerous to his self-integrity than taking on the fight. I'll use his story to take us to the end of the chapter. Matthew tells this part of his story because he was surprised by the strong energy that emerged in him to take on a battle he believed he had no hope of winning. In his view, he had a choice between exiting with dignity or staying without it. Something in him decided that his dignity was too important to give up for the sake of a job.

When I sat across from the head of our harassment committee and heard her repeat the ultimatum that my adversaries had given to her – "Tell Matthew to step aside or we will have him removed" – I had two energies come up in me. One was nervous energy. I knew I wasn't clever enough to outwit these people. I knew I didn't have their status or position. I knew that any fight against them would end badly for me – everything in our system was set in their favour. All sorts of questions played out in my mind. Who would help me? Who could I count on? Would the founder live up to his promises? Would I be abandoned?

I worried about what sort of job I could get afterwards. My expertise is narrow, and my family situation meant that I wasn't very mobile. Would we have to move? Would I find a new position that suited me better? That earned me a good salary? That would help me feel valued? That would help me grow?

All of these concerns were strong and real and almost over-whelming. But another energy in me was even more powerful. It also showed up that day in the office of the head of our harassment committee, feeling her gentle nudges encouraging me to step aside from the fight. It's hard to describe, but I think of it as an energy that was beckoning me forward toward a better me. It asked me to consider the cost of my compromises. It showed me the limitation of that part of me that wanted to please. It made me wonder how miserable I might become if I submitted. It also gave me a hint about what might lay ahead for me if I were courageous enough to stand up for my values. It didn't make any promises. It only told me that it might be better to step into the unknown than to drink poison, no matter who was trying to convince me that the poison tasted good. I'm still exploring this energy in me. It's more concerned about my growth than my comfort, so it's a good energy to know.

SUMMARY

Our conscious mind and our unconscious mind each have their own intelligence and their own language. We work at our best when we understand and use them both. We rely on the rationality and sharp thinking of our conscious mind to carry us through most of our leadership work, but the instincts and energies that sit in our unconscious are just as essential, especially when we step into transitional space.

Our unconscious is the container of all the instincts that are programmed into us as a social species that evolved in a challenging environment. It guides how we behave in social hierarchies, how we respond to threats, and how we compete for resources. It gives us the desire for personal agency and for community with others. It arms us with a host of protective emotions and generative emotions so that we can guard ourselves from danger and so that we can grow. These ancient instincts are alive and well in our lives and in our leadership.

Our unconscious holds the essential human anxieties of death, isolation, freedom and meaning. These anxieties are imbedded in human vulnerability, and they are uncomfortable. We can try to avoid thinking about them. Or we can openly and honestly explore what they mean for us. Our leadership gives us a rich platform for honest exploration.

Our unconscious holds the compromises we've made to be acceptable to the people around us, the parts of ourselves that we hide because we don't like them, or because we are afraid the people around us won't like them. It also holds our sense of who we would like to become, an image of the best version of ourselves living the fullest possible life.

Like any significant transitions in life, leadership transitions take us into in-between space. In-between space encourages us to examine the helpful and unhelpful ways our instincts show up, the mindful or forgetful ways we wrestle with our anxieties, and the extent to which we are living the best version of our lives. Leadership transitions are rich opportunities for us to explore all of these aspects of our unconscious.

In Chapter 3, I'll describe what post-traumatic growth and narrative psychology say about how we grow through life's transitions. Post-traumatic growth explains that even our most difficult transitions lead to profound growth when they help us develop a wiser narrative of the world and of how we operate in it. Narrative psychology helps us understand better the role of our narrative world. Both have important wisdom to share with leaders who are taking on the task of significant change.

Before we turn to Chapter 3, take a few minutes to answer three questions. Write whatever comes to mind. Don't worry if it makes sense, and don't worry about editing. Avoid bullet points; the rider speaks in bullet points. The elephant wants to tell a story.

1. Think of a time in your leadership when you were anxious, angry or afraid. What was the situation? In what ways might deep instincts for survival have been the source of your emotions, trying to guide you to safety? Were any of our usual survival instincts – flight, fight, freeze, fawn and faint – at play? Once you sketch out that story, answer an additional question: How well did your instincts serve you?

2. Remember a time in your leadership when you felt you were at your very best. What happened? Why was it a peak experience for you? Try to remember details of the story. Who was involved? What role did you play in the story? What emotions were at play in you and in the people around you?

3. Think of a time in your leadership when you felt uncomfortable with a request or direction from someone more senior than you in the organizational hierarchy. How did you respond? How do you wish you had responded? If there is a difference between your two answers, what is the difference telling you?

CHAPTER 3

WISE NARRATIVES

WHAT HAPPENS WHEN OUR MENTAL OPERATING SYSTEMS BREAK DOWN

We are all tellers of tales, and we seek to provide our scattered and often confusing experiences with a sense of coherence by arranging the episodes of our lives. Starting in late adolescence, we manufacture our dramatic personal myths by selectively mining some experiences and neglecting or forgetting others.

- DAN P. MCADAMS,
THE STORIES WE LIVE BY

Ash, Matthew and I had some things in common. We were all senior leaders. We had successful leadership careers behind us. We believed in what we were doing. Thanks to our success, we had all reached a point in our work when we were asked to take on more challenging roles. We were all asked to trust the organizations in which we operated. And we were all badly shaken by the experience that followed.

In Chapter 2, we learned that our unconscious minds run much of the show in our daily lives and in our leadership. We learned that we are unconsciously driven by age-old instincts that fit imperfectly in our modern world. We learned that our unconscious minds search for answers to important questions about what it means to be human, and that we often accept easy and comforting answers to these questions to avoid taking on the hard work of finding more meaningful answers. Finally, we learned that our unconscious minds are keepers of all the many ways in which we repress our desires, emotions, beliefs, values and wounds so that we are acceptable to the world around us, and that we reach a point in our lives when we become tired of our compromises. If we are willing to take on the hard work of understanding what's going on beneath the surface, we turn toward the task of growing.

We have two more schools of psychology to cover before we turn to Part Two. They are the psychology of post-traumatic growth and narrative psychology. Both schools highlight the importance of our narrative worlds, and both have special wisdom to share about how our minds work when we are in transition.

THE CASE FOR POST-TRAUMA/ POST-TRANSITION GROWTH: RE-ORDERING OUR INNER WORLDS

When Ash described her leadership experience as *"an assault on her soul,"* and as *"psychological torture,"* my first reaction was: *"Yes, that's it! That's my experience too!"* My second reaction was: *"Really? It's only leadership. No one is dying here."* Despite my skepticism and probably because my own leadership transition was so surprisingly difficult, after talking to Ash I turned my research to understanding what mechanisms might have provoked such strong emotional reactions in us. That search quickly led me to the field of psychological trauma, and the growing field of post-traumatic growth.

Trauma is an overused word in today's culture. The frequency with which people who live out their lives as social media performances referencing their many traumas has cheapened the meaning of the traumatic experience. It turns out, however, that clinical practice in trauma has been shifting its own definitions. When I started a literature search in trauma and trauma recovery, I assumed that trauma happened on the battlefield or through equally horrible (and equally rare, I hoped) physical and psychological experiences. I imagined that the symptoms of trauma – what we officially began to call post-traumatic stress disorder (PTSD) in 1980 – were also rare. I was only partly right.

It's true that clinical research in trauma owes its beginnings to work with profoundly destabilized people. Trauma research began with clinical attempts to help these walking wounded return to functional lives. It's also true that more recent clinical work has revised the definition of trauma to include any and all experiences that might lead to hyper-alertness to threat and exaggerated threat responses. Two founding researchers in clinical work in post-traumatic growth, Lawrence Calhoun and Richard Tedeschi, observed that both these responses were linked to any experience in which certain core beliefs – what they called core narratives and what other researchers call core schemas or assumptions – are shattered. They broaden the definition of trauma to include any major stressor that leads to hyper threat awareness and exaggerated threat response:

> We use the terms trauma, crisis, major stressor and related terms as essentially synonymous expressions to describe very difficult circumstances that significantly challenge or invalidate important components of the person's assumptive world.[25]

Heightened psychological responses happen when core components of our worldview and self-view are broken by experience. All it takes for us to become hyper-alert to threat and to exaggerate our threat response mechanisms is for an event or an experience to shatter our way of thinking about how the world works and destroy our beliefs about what we need to do to operate successfully in it.

In the last chapter I mentioned existential psychology's observation that we tend to protect our core beliefs vigorously because losing them leaves us without a way to make sense of the world. Post-traumatic growth agrees. We protect our core beliefs so vigorously because losing them threatens our psychological health. We are traumatized when the load-bearing walls of our core belief systems crumble under the weight of any experience that invalidates them. We are programmed to treat confusion as threat, and there is no greater confusion than the confusion that comes when the inner maps we use to understand and navigate through our worlds don't work any more.

Once I understood how clinical work thinks about trauma, its link to leadership became clear. Try this experiment. Think about your leadership in terms of what you believe to be true about the world you live in, about the organization you serve, about the behaviour of the people around you, and about your own ability. Make a list of your beliefs and imagine how you would react if any or all of these beliefs were shattered.

Here's a short version of what my list would have looked like when I began my leadership transition:

- The people who asked me to take on the new role actually want me to do the work they've asked me to do.
- Good behaviour is rewarded, and bad behaviour is punished, and the opposite isn't true.
- A long history of achieving excellent results will earn me some freedom to do what I think is right, even if what I think is right challenges some powerful people.
- Leaders don't mob good performers.
- I am capable of doing what I've been asked to do.
- I can count on the support of the many people that I have actively supported over the years.
- Boards pay attention to what's going on in the organizations they govern, and our board will take corrective action when they see how poor leadership is corrupting our organization.
- The health of the organization matters more than pleasing one or two bad actors.
- My work is for a worthy cause.
- Organizations should care about the quality of their leadership.

Each of these beliefs was invalidated by the experience that followed my acceptance of the new leadership role. Post-traumatic growth clinicians would claim that the psychological pain of my experience came from the loss of these important beliefs. They would also say that my pain would be amplified, even traumatic, if any of these beliefs were essential to how I looked at the world. It turns out that several of them were.[26]

PAYING ATTENTION TO OUR CORE NARRATIVES

Take another look at your list of core leadership beliefs. Try to identify two or three that are essential to you. Trauma researchers would predict that your most essential beliefs fall into one of three categories. Beliefs that fall within these three categories are the most difficult for us to lose, even (and especially) when experience tells us that they are no longer valid. The three categories are:

1. *Benevolence:* belief that the world is benevolent, at least toward me.
2. *Fairness:* belief that good things happen to good people, and if I am very good, bad things won't happen to me.
3. *Self-worth:* belief that I am a good person.[27]

Every one of the beliefs in my list falls into at least one of these three categories, which means that when my experience assaulted each of them, I was vulnerable to a deep defensive reaction. Trauma researchers would not be surprised with how Ash, Matthew and I reacted in the face of our experiences. They would not find it strange that each of us exhibited the confusion and exaggerated response that typically indicates psychological harm. They certainly would not be surprised that so many of the leaders we support during their most important and challenging career transitions are nudging up against the edge of traumatic experience. Many of them are confronted with the destruction of their core beliefs about a benevolent world, about fairness and about self-worth when they step into the chaos of their work and encounter the very human surprises and perceived betrayals that can come during leadership transitions.

It isn't hard to find examples from our practice.[28] Here are a few:

There's Nicolas, who worked his way up to leading the largest of three businesses in the company he serves, only to feel that being a leader requires him to become someone he doesn't like being (benevolence). He senses that his contribution in the company's executive committee meetings is limited to reporting his division's latest financial results (fairness). He doesn't believe that this positioning treats him well (benevolence) or is appropriate given all the hard work he dedicates to helping the company be successful (fairness). In some ways he feels like the only child in a room full of impressive adults during these meetings (self-worth). He believes that he is very well paid, probably more than he deserves, and he isn't sure why he was chosen for his current role (self-worth). The person he replaced in the role was a legend in the company, loved by everyone, and Nicolas isn't sure if he can live up to that person's reputation (self-worth).

There's also David, a newly appointed CEO who manages to guide his global company through the initial stages of COVID-19 only to find that the board is being used by the owning family to manoeuvre through strategies that have more to do with awkward family politics than with the health of the business. No matter what success David manages to achieve despite the challenging economic environment, it isn't quite enough for the board (benevolence, fairness).

More and more of David's time is pulled away from navigating the organization through an increasingly chaotic world to attend to weakening board relationships, a difficult task when David suspects that at least a few board members aren't interested in his success (fairness).

There's Caroline, who after 25 years of hard work takes on an important marketing role in her company's most significant region. No sooner has Caroline settled into the work than a new CEO steps in with a fresh team of senior executives, a new culture and new ways of working that seem counter to the organization's health and Caroline's ways of working (benevolence). Suddenly, unqualified people are promoted to important positions because they say the right things, slick presentations replace the hard work of what it takes to win in the marketplace, and Caroline's vast experience becomes a liability (*old-school*) rather than an asset (*experience*) (benevolence, fairness, self-worth).

And Alex, a new member of the management team of a financial services business that has successfully jumped the hurdle of a difficult restructuring and transformation. Alex comes from outside the organization. He is told that part of why the organization hired him, in addition to his technical and leadership skills, is because he is 'refreshingly different.' By that, Alex assumes senior leaders mean that they appreciated his openness, his transparency and his dry humour. That is, until a member of the team he inherited who was close to his predecessor lodges a complaint against Alex because he took offense to one or two of Alex's 'refreshingly different' comments. Alex suddenly finds himself at the centre of a secretive and punitive process that seems to assume that he is guilty of offenses that he doesn't quite understand but that he's pretty sure he didn't commit, especially since they seem to be offenses that are contrary to his most deeply held values (benevolence, fairness). Alex is kept in the dark about the process, but not about the results. The accuser walks away with a healthy financial settlement, Alex is punished (fairness), warned about his behaviour (benevolence, fairness) even as he is praised for his performance, and left wondering how he could be treated so strangely by an organization he is committed to growing (fairness, self-worth).

The most remarkable thing about these stories is how common they are. Leaders at all levels often find themselves immersed in the kind of profound chaos that challenges important assumptions they've made about the world and about their work. While not all leaders will experience these circumstances as traumatic, at some point in our careers almost all leaders edge into territory where a heightened threat response is justified. This possibility goes with the territory of leading at the edge, whether or not trauma, in a clinical sense, takes place. The importance of post-traumatic growth research is that its wisdom guides us through any important transition, not just the traumatizing ones.

THE CASE FOR NARRATIVE: UNDERSTANDING THE STORIES WE LIVE BY

Post-traumatic growth has three important insights for transitioning leaders.

First, it shows us that even the most destabilizing experiences can become territory for profound personal development. With destruction comes an opportunity to rebuild something better.

Second, it tells us that the first move toward growth comes from turning what post-traumatic growth clinicians call intrusive rumination into intentional rumination. Growth happens when we take the time and effort to tell the story of our experience rather than let our unconscious reflexes tell the story for us. Growth happens when the rider and the elephant work together to make sense of their experience.

Third, intentionally exploring our destabilizing experiences helps us create what post-traumatic growth clinicians call the wise narrative of our experience, of our work and of us. Creating this wise narrative is the essential step of personal growth after a destabilizing experience. I'll spend some time explaining each of these observations before turning to Part Two and the practice of leading at the edge.

NECESSARY DESTRUCTION

Remember from Chapter 1 that the field of post-traumatic growth grew out of an observation that psychologically challenging experiences lead to one of three outcomes. One outcome is common but not good. The second outcome is better. And the third outcome is best.

The first outcome is that the experience leaves us less than we were. Think of the traumatic event from which the victim struggles to recover. In wartime trauma, these are the soldiers whose threat response mechanisms are so triggered by loud noise that they are unable to operate effectively in public life. In leadership, we think of leaders whose experience of leading is so confusing and so full of betrayal that they lose their confidence and their enthusiasm for the task of leadership. This leadership outcome happens more than we might think: a common theme of our work is the struggle to maintain confidence when the world around us doesn't operate as we expect it to.

The second outcome is when the experience rattles us temporarily, but we somehow recover our previous functionality. In these cases, we are resilient. As I mentioned in Chapter 1, resilience is a good outcome. It is such a good outcome that in the decades that followed the first research into trauma and trauma response, resilience was the only outcome that mattered. We are in good shape if we can bounce back from the many challenges that we face in our leadership. We are doing well if our optimism, our hope and our confidence remain intact despite the many disappointments, frustrations and betrayals we might face as we try to lead. We are in great shape if even our worst experiences don't diminish us in any essential way.

There's a better outcome. This is the outcome that prompted the first explorations of what became the field of post-traumatic growth. The better outcome is when the burnt ground left in the wake of our devastating experiences becomes fertile earth for the emergence of a new us. Calhoun and Tedeschi refer to this phenomenon as "the experience of positive change that the individual experiences as a result of the struggle with a traumatic event."[29] The field grew out of the observation that for some people, the same challenging experiences that force us to rethink our worldviews and belief systems are the experiences that enable us to break out of old limitations and grow. Translating their work to the world of leadership, post-traumatic growth practice would say that any of our leadership experiences that push us to the edge of our existing mental schemas or that challenge how we think about the world and how we think about ourselves are experiences that we can use for our own growth.[30]

CONSCIOUS NARRATIVES

What separates growth from resilience or destruction? The first step in the growth journey is to understand what happens to our inner narrative-making function when an experience overwhelms us. Think of our narrative-making function as how our rider and elephant try to make sense of our experiences. As discussed in the first chapter, our unconscious mind is our most active story-maker: when it comes to making sense of experience, the elephant leads. Our elephant's leadership role is especially evident during our most overwhelming experiences, when our deepest instincts for survival and our most embedded coping mechanisms are triggered into action. Under stress, our elephants run where they want, driven by ancient and unconscious drives. Post-traumatic growth researchers refer to this tendency for our unconscious minds to take over when we are most challenged as 'intrusive rumination': that is, our thoughts and fears intrude on our minds. These thoughts are survival mechanisms on overdrive, desperate to keep us safe in the face of the overwhelming confusion that comes when our core narratives fall apart.

The path to growth starts when we decide to become intentional about the stories we tell ourselves about our experiences. The turn toward intentionality is a way for the rider and elephant to make sense together, with curiosity and with a desire to explore experience, even difficult experience, for the wisdom we can learn from it.

The narrative turn toward intentionality isn't easy. Intentionality isn't a matter of telling ourselves that we will shut down the parts of our unconscious mind that are filling our heads with intrusive thoughts. Our elephants go where their instinct or fear tells them to go. It takes time and effort to calm them. And, it turns out, we can't just rely on our riders to sooth our elephants when they're provoked by threat. Trauma researchers note that the same trauma that enrages the elephant weakens the driver. In the face of overwhelming threat, our psychological energy leaves the rider so that it can serve the elephant. Trauma researcher Bessel van der Kolk notes:

> For a hundred years or more, every textbook of psychology and psychotherapy has advised that some method of talking about distressing feelings can resolve them. However, as we've seen, the experience of trauma itself gets in the way of being able to do that. No matter how much insight and understanding we develop, the rational brain is basically impotent to talk the emotional brain out of its own reality.[31]

This reflex to direct our psychological resources to our unconscious mind makes sense for short-term survival: when the tiger attacks, it's unhealthy to ruminate over the tiger's motives. But the implications of the reflex are significant. Trauma not only destroys the load-bearing walls of our narrative world; it also destroys our ability to create new ones. "It is enormously difficult to organize one's traumatic experiences into a coherent account – a narrative with a beginning, a middle and an end," van der Kolk writes. But it's the exploration of the experience and the translation of it into a structured and insightful narrative – a wise narrative – that plays the essential role in turning our edge experiences into wisdom.

WISE NARRATIVE AND ITS TREASURES

What do we mean by wise narratives? Think of the wise narrative as the story that comes out of an honest and reflective exploration of the wisdom that can be taken from our destabilizing experiences. Calhoun and Tedeschi, our two ground-breakers in the field of post-traumatic growth, illustrate the process that leads to wise narratives in the following way:[32]

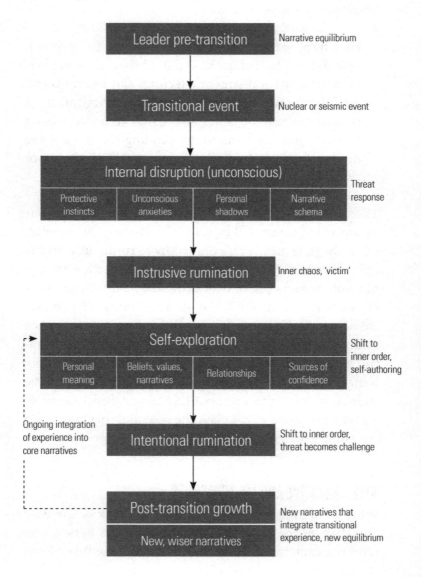

We start with who we are as a person and as a leader, complete with our set of beliefs and assumptions about ourselves and about how leadership works, before we step into transitional space. This is me with the set of ten beliefs I had when I stepped into my new role, with my history of success and with my assumptions about how the people around me would respond when I took on the work I was asked to do.

Next comes what post-traumatic growth clinicians call a seismic event, the edge experiences that leaders sometimes face in the course of their work. These are the experiences that test, and sometimes destroy, the mental models and belief systems that we use to navigate our way in the world. The seismic event challenges us in three interconnected ways. First, we need to deal with our emotional distress. At the same time, we face the confusion that comes from the absence of our guiding beliefs and the sudden meaninglessness of the goals that used to inspire us to action. And we need to face both of those challenges without the core narratives that once helped us navigate our way through life. We are, in a psychological sense, without an inner compass.

Our unconscious minds respond to this threatening confusion with an automatic blend of instincts and anxieties. Our protective emotions take over. Whatever fears and angers we've soothed beneath the surface of our old narratives are stirred awake. We are initially helpless to steer our elephant in any conscious direction.

With effort and time, we calm down our unconscious reactions and start to make sense of our experience. The elephant breathes again, and the rider begins to regain some sense of influence over our actions. Disclosure helps because it forces us to put form to our inner confusion. As we disengage from our old beliefs and question the goals that matter most to us, we start to feel a growing sense of authorship over the story of our experience. Our intrusive reactions recede, perhaps just a little, but a little is often enough for our riders to regain enough strength to engage the elephant in an honest exploration of our experience. We then start the challenging journey of finding new ways to look to the world. Through intentional exploration, our rider and our elephant start to create new and wiser narratives that integrate all that the experience has taught us about who we are, about how the world really works and about what is most important to us.

Calhoun and Tedeschi's insights explain why Ash, Matthew and I were so badly shaken by our leadership transitions. Each of us had been well-served by our old narratives. Each of us had some of these narratives destroyed by our leadership experiences. Each of us suffered through the pain of their loss. We all struggled to understand how it was that our assumptions and expectations played out so differently than our narratives would have suggested: sometimes organizations do scapegoat leaders rather than face up to their cultural shortcomings; sometimes senior leaders do mob even the most capable and well-intentioned employees; sometimes high-status players are more than willing to sacrifice others so that they can maintain their privileged place in the hierarchy. With time and guidance, however, we were all willing to explore these narratives and see what we could construct in the aftermath of their deconstruction.

Tedeschi and Calhoun's process for post-traumatic growth explained how we were each able to turn a painful journey into a profound one. Their clinical insights into the narratives that matter most when it comes to our psychological wellbeing helped us to focus our growth work. For that story, we turn to Part Two: The Leader's Compass.

"

By working on the narrative, the client comes to appreciate that there are various points of view from which events can be appreciated and understood. These perspectives represent opportunities to recast a traumatic event and its aftermath into constructive stories that can be used in the years ahead, forming a framework for a purposeful and satisfying life post-trauma.

"

- LAURENCE CALHOUN & RICHARD TEDESCHI,
POSTTRAUMATIC GROWTH IN CLINICAL PRACTICE

SUMMARY

Each of us relies on a set of assumptions and beliefs to navigate our way through our worlds. These beliefs help us make decisions. They guide our behaviours. They nudge us in one direction or another as we make our way through the daily labyrinth of our lives. They are often formed unconsciously and sit within us untested and unchanged, especially if they sit high in the hierarchy of our internal belief systems. We defend these beliefs vigorously because our sense of psychological safety relies on them.

Important transitions test our core beliefs. Sometimes difficult transitions destroy them, and we aren't able to build new ones. Sometimes our core beliefs remain intact through a challenging transition. In these cases, our beliefs give us the resilience we need to withstand potentially traumatic experiences. In some cases, though, stepping into transitional space destroys some of our core beliefs and we are able to reconstruct new, wiser beliefs in their place. This reconstruction process is at the heart of post-transitions growth. Every time we step into an important life transition, we have an opportunity to test our core narratives and replace them with wiser ones. We construct wise narratives when we are able to examine our experiences intentionally and consciously so that we can derive wisdom from them. We look at the narrative-making process in Part Two. Before we go there, take a few minutes to sketch out answers to the following questions. Answering them will help prepare you for the material we will cover in the coming chapters.

1. Think of a time when a destabilizing experience taught you something important about yourself or about the world around you. Maybe you moved, or changed to a different school, or an important relationship changed. What happened? How did the experience help you grow? If you could live your life over again, would you repeat the experience, assuming that giving up the experience would mean giving up the growth?

2. Identify a belief that was once essential to you but has now changed. What was the old belief? Where did it come from? What wiser belief has replaced it? Where did that belief come from? How difficult was it for you to change the belief?

GROWTH FROM CHAOS

"

Resistance to the organized mass can be effected only by the man who is as well organized in his individuality as the mass itself.

"

- CARL JUNG,
THE UNDISCOVERED SELF

Sometimes difficult stories have happy endings.

After many months of doubt, I was able to pivot my PhD work toward a more meaningful topic. I found a workplace that welcomed me. I was able to discover which developmental work I liked enough to justify the hard work required to do it well. I settled into a new career that built on my experience and satisfied my deep desire to make more of a difference. My wise narrative turned toward work that I thought was important. It explained the behaviour of the people around me during my experience as the kind of behaviour that sometimes happens when our shadows show up at work. I may have been a victim of their manipulation, but the wise narrative of the experience wasn't a narrative of victimhood. It was a story of burning away the old so that a better new could emerge.

I wasn't alone. Although Ash's story unfolded over a much longer period, her experience prompted her to champion the cause of mental health at work. She brings a profound credibility to the effort as a scientist and as someone who has lived through, explored and made sense out of the 'psychological torture' of her time at the cross-roads.[33] She has taken on the task of making sure that organizations understand the terrible costs of performance when it comes at the end of the whip of toxic leadership. The current attention we're giving to workplace burnout suggests that Ash has her work cut out for her.

Given what we now know about working through challenging transitions, leaders have every reason to believe that even the most difficult transitions can be sources of great wisdom. In Chapter 3, I shared four brief cases of leaders whose core beliefs in benevolence, fairness and self-worth were shattered by their leadership work. In all four cases, the leader managed to make the pivot away from intrusive, unconscious narrative to narrative wisdom. Each of these cases is instructive.

In the case of Nicolas, the leader of an organization's largest business unit who felt instrumentalized by his organization, dissatisfaction with his sense of himself at work pivoted when he began to think differently about what success really means for him. After some important exploration into his driving desire to win, Nicolas understood that his old definitions of winning no longer worked. A wiser story of what it means to win needed to mean more than commercial success. It needed to include a broader range of personal and professional goals, including an important but long-buried goal to help the people around him grow. A more nuanced definition of success lightened the weight of the leadership burden Nicolas felt he was carrying. He started to experiment with a more optimistic leadership style that amplified his energy for experimentation and growth. As of this writing, Nicolas is a candidate to be successor to the chief executive.

David, the CEO of the organization that had successfully navigated through the considerable trials of COVID-19, had a slightly more difficult story. After careful exploration of the wise narrative he wanted to live through his leadership – a story that he knew included a sense of collective ambition among the senior leadership and board – David understood that his current organization wasn't the right stage. He negotiated a polite departure that freed him to spend more time with his family as he searched for more welcoming organizations. After a few months, David secured the senior leadership role in an organization that has proved to be a better stage for the honest living of his wise leadership narrative.

Caroline, the marketing leader who after 25 years of service felt the organization's culture shift away from her, has remained with the company. She stayed true to her belief in hard work and direct communication over the shifting culture's new appreciation for slickness. Caroline's wise narrative was one that found honest answers to the question of what was really unfolding in her work. She acknowledged that sometimes new CEOs do want to have an immediate impact, and that they often bring with them new ideas and new ways of working and new people, all of which might feel unfamiliar or wrong or destructive to someone whose convictions have formed through more than two decades of honest effort. Caroline prepared herself to leave the company because she understood that her wise leadership narrative might no longer have a place in the organization. As it turned out, though, her hard work, insights and unwillingness to say things she didn't believe attracted the attention of the organization's new senior leaders. Before long, Caroline was asked to leave her marketing role so that she could lead the company's largest division in its largest market. She still struggles with the organization's culture shifts, but she is learning to manage the tension between what was and what is becoming so that it doesn't overwhelm her natural optimism. And she appreciates the positive feedback her honesty and transparency earns her from her team, her line managers and her peers.

And finally we get to Alex, the leader who came into a new organization with enthusiasm only to find himself accused of and punished for behaviour he didn't believe he committed. Alex's wise narrative became one in which he was able to express his disappointment to the organization's leaders clearly, forcefully and maturely. He reimagined his leadership narrative as one that demanded respect from the company he supported, just as the company expected respect from him. Alex pivoted away from his anger and disappointment once he understood that he could flourish only when his relationship with the company became an adult-to-adult relationship rather than one in which he would compromise important parts of himself in order to get along. Alex continues to work in the leadership team of the company. He enjoys his ability to express his natural enthusiasm, perhaps in a slightly more nuanced way than before but with just as much energy.

If you see some patterns in these wise narratives, you might be recognizing the same narrative tendencies that clinical psychologists noticed in their research into post-traumatic growth. Clinical work with people who suffered traumatic experiences shows that happy endings come through intentional exploration of difficult experiences so that we can extract wisdom from them. It goes a step further, however. It also helps us understand which narratives seem to play the most important roles in guiding us through our edge experiences. Tedeschi and Calhoun mention three categories of narratives that seem to provide us with psychological stability and the possibility for profound growth: *a changed sense of oneself, a changed sense of relationships with others,* and *a changed philosophy of life*. Narratives in all three of these categories play a particularly important role in our sense of who we are and in how we can best operate in the world.[34] The researchers note six common narratives that fit under these three categories. Think of these as the stories that people tell about how they have grown once they've been through the crucible of transition. Since these narratives are at the heart of the Leader's Compass work we will cover in Part Two, I'll explain each of the six in some detail. The six are:

1. I am much stronger than I ever imagined.
2. I have strengthened and deepened the relationships that matter most to me.

3. I feel much freer to express my emotions.
4. I have prioritized what is really important to me.
5. I appreciate the small things in my life much more.
6. I pay more attention to the meaning and purpose of my life.

I AM MUCH STRONGER THAN I EVER IMAGINED

The first wise narrative is a narrative of personal strength. A common realization of people who grow because of difficult transitions is that they recognize how strong they are. Out of their confusion comes a newfound understanding of their own abilities and inner resources. A good example of this kind of narrative came out of a conversation I had with a global chief human resources officer yesterday. Although our conversation was mainly focused on the work we're doing to help the company's CEO designate to prepare for his transition into the role, at the end of our conversation he mentioned to me that the circumstances of his private life had shifted for the better. He and his wife are in the process of divorcing. He has been carrying the heavy burden of this change over the past months, but something had recently shifted for him. "I am proud of how we have all managed the situation," he explained, referring to the way he and his soon-to-be ex-wife were able to navigate their way through the difficult changes in their relationship. "I am proud of us. I understand now how strong I am. If I can manage my way through this, I can manage my way through anything."

This theme of understanding our own strength only because it has been tested, perhaps for the first time, is often a key part of a leader's wise narrative. Leadership provides us with no shortage of transitional experiences to test us. Emerging from the most difficult of them with a new understanding of our inner resourcefulness enables us to look ahead with an appreciation that while we may be more vulnerable to the random punches that life might throw at us, we are also much more capable of dealing with them than we once imagined.

I HAVE STRENGTHENED AND DEEPENED THE RELATIONSHIPS THAT MATTER MOST TO ME

The second wise narrative is the narrative of deepened connection. Tedeschi and Calhoun describe how trauma tends to sharpen our focus, including our focus on the quality of our relationships with the people who matter most to us. This was true in my story, both in terms of my relationship with the organization that employed me and in terms of my relationships outside of work. At work, much of my energy had gone into pleasing the people who I thought I needed to please. I depended on my work for a sense of status, importance and security – all the things that existential psychology says are too important to hand over to the care of an organization. It was, to be sure, an unbalanced relationship. Transitions sometimes teach us that it can be difficult to develop high-quality human relationships at work. The lesson is a painful one. Of all the wisdom I took from my edge experience, understanding that our relationships with our leaders, our colleagues and our organizations work best when they are adult-to-adult relationships was the most important.

I FEEL MUCH FREER TO EXPRESS MY EMOTIONS

The third wise narrative is the narrative of emotional openness. This narrative is related to the narrative above about nurturing deep relationships with the people who matter most to us. One dimension of relationship depth is honesty, and one dimension of honesty is being open with how we feel, even when sharing how we feel seems risky. Tedeschi and Calhoun describe the wise narrative of emotional transparency in the following way:

> There can be a greater sense of freedom to talk about one's thoughts and feelings, but also a greater sense of allowing oneself to let others *see* the feelings and emotions. The encounter with suffering can lead people to be more honest, at least with trusted others, about how they think and feel, and to experience greater ease in expressing themselves emotionally to others.[35]

Our transitions tend to elicit strong emotional responses in us. To make sense of these emotions, we must explore them. The process of exploring our emotions, especially our most negative emotions, helps us become more comfortable with them. The more comfortable we are with them, the more comfortable we are with sharing them.

It's important to note that there's a critical shift in emotional expression that comes during our transitional experiences. The shift follows the post-traumatic growth pivot from intrusive rumination to intentional rumination. The more we are in the grip of our edge experiences, the more explosive, raw and vivid our emotions tend to be. A wiser narrative of these emotions comes after exploration and intentional rumination. I remember with embarrassment when my own emotions boiled over in one of our leadership team meetings.

Just before the meeting, one of my colleagues told me that our line manager was working hard to ruin the reputation of a leader I'd just hired on to my team. During the meeting, I remember hammering my fist on the table and swearing after a slight provocation from the line manager.

It was not my proudest leadership moment, but it was a good example of how unexplored emotions might be better left inside rather than expressed in their rawest form. Since that experience, I've paid much more attention when negative emotions want to be expressed.[36]

I HAVE PRIORITIZED WHAT IS REALLY IMPORTANT TO ME

The fourth wise narrative is the narrative of how we choose to spend our time. Tedeschi and Calhoun tell a story of reprioritization in the opening chapter of *Posttraumatic Growth in Clinical Practice*. I'll share it here because it is a good example of the kinds of shifting that we see in our developmental work with executives:

> A young man who had just turned 30 made an appointment because he was very depressed and he said he knew the reason for his great sadness. His main goal in life and his top priority for how to live was to be a millionaire by the time he was 30 and he had fallen short of his goal – he had amassed only "$750,000 in liquid assets" by his 30th birthday. The failure to achieve his chosen life goal had led him to great despair. Maybe his priorities needed a little shifting. Shifts in priorities are common in people who have faced major life crises. Perhaps the young man needed the somewhat frank, and perhaps a little harsh, advice from a marathon runner who had been treated for cancer. "It may sound brutal, but maybe everybody should have a little cancer to help change them."[37]

I heard similar comments about the seduction of unwise priorities years ago when I worked briefly with a group of managing directors in a global financial services organization. They had all completed a series of assessments, and I was asked to review the results with each of them. I used the occasion to explore what they each found meaningful in their lives and in their work. They all explained to me how important their families were to them, but when I asked them what success looked like, almost all of them told me a version of "I'll know I am successful when I make as much money as my boss's boss." Never mind that focusing your life on achieving such a moveable target comes with its own ironies: their comments didn't align well with all the stories they told about the importance of their lives outside of work. Tedeschi and Calhoun share another story that might have helped these executives:

> Such changed priorities are reflected in the experiences of a highly placed executive who had a heart attack. He had been a collegiate athlete and had never been seriously ill a day in his life. The cardiac event changed him. After he was released from the hospital, he altered his work schedule to spend more time with his children, aged three and six. The importance of corporate advancement was no longer the single most important focus of his life – his family was.[38]

Of course, maintaining a healthy balance between life at work and life outside of work needs constant attention. Sometimes compromises are appropriate. The important point here is that the wise narrative of how we prioritize our activities in life comes from intentional reflection. We can become so busy doing what we think we should be doing that we are distracted from considering whether we are really doing the right things. We don't always need to pay more attention to our lives outside of work. We do always need to pay attention to whether or not our priorities reflect a wise narrative of our lives and our leadership.

I APPRECIATE THE SMALL THINGS IN MY LIFE MUCH MORE

The fifth wise narrative is the narrative of our sources of joy and fulfilment. Our transitions are sometimes so all-consuming that we neglect the activities and habits that are essential to our lives. When I was so worried about dangers at work, I left no psychological space for the countless things in my life for which I could be grateful and which replenished me. It's a normal reflex: when we are under threat, our instinct is to deal with the threat. The wise narrative of giving due importance to the small things in our lives helps us remember, how-ever, that our lives are more than our work and that threats need to be put into wise perspective.

Tedeschi and Calhoun suggest that the increased appreciation for the small things in life is part of an increased appreciation for life itself. They note that greater appreciation for life usually comes after one's trauma has been life-threatening – serious cancer, a heart attack, exposure to the possibility of physical violence, for example. It begs the question: Why would this wise narrative play a role in our edge experiences as leaders, when our lives aren't really in danger? There are two answers. First, it's important to remember that the urges and instincts that sit in us can react with just as much vigour to threats to our security as they would have in our tribal life thousands of years ago. Second, given the rising rates of serious mental health issues in organizational life, it's wise to remember that some-times organizations do put us in profound physical and mental danger.[39]

I PAY MORE ATTENTION TO THE MEANING AND PURPOSE OF MY LIFE

The final wise narrative that sometimes emerges from edge experiences has a spiritual dimension to it. Calhoun and Tedeschi use the metaphor of 'thin places' to describe how traumatic experiences can prompt us to ask ourselves important questions of meaning in our lives. Thin places are liminal spaces. They are the places that connect us with other worlds. Anthropologists write about the importance of the liminal spaces between who we were and who we are becoming when we pass through important life transitions. They connect us more closely to our deepest desires and most profound sense of meaning. They are also places of creativity, exploration, of being unbounded by the old rules and unencumbered by old beliefs that might once have constrained us.

Calhoun and Tedeschi observe:

> For some people, the experience of a major life crisis can represent a metaphorical thin place, where the confrontation with suffering or mortality makes them aware of more spiritual things, or makes them more likely to engage with the fundamental existential questions of meaning in life.[40]

They also note:

> It is important not to equate the metaphor of thin places with an exclusively religious meaning. Even atheists or agnostics may experience their encounter with loss or trauma as an existential thin place. Their confrontation is not with questions about God or the religious meaning of suffering, but about the fundamental existential questions that are not limited to worldviews. Questions such as: What should I do with

the rest of my life? What sense can I make out of what is happening and will happen? and What purpose, if any, is there to all this?[41]

The importance of our purpose narrative explains why so much of the modern self-help leadership literature encourages leaders to articulate their sense of purpose. This process usually focuses on creating a personal purpose statement that somehow contains the deepest meaning of the leader's life and work, which the leader can use as a source of inspiration and direction. I've been involved in this kind of purpose work both on the receiving end and in helping executives find deeper meaning in their work. While I agree that understanding your personal sources of meaning is critical for a well-lived life, the experience of integrating post-traumatic growth work into leadership development work shows that our sense of purpose is nuanced, malleable and resistant to concrete definition. It can't be contained in a purpose statement.

The four chapters of Part Two integrate post-trauma growth narratives into four categories. Each category represents a point on the leader's inner compass. The chapters ahead help you develop a wise narrative in each compass point.

In Chapter 4, we will turn toward meaning and purpose. Think of it as the North point of the compass.

Chapter 5 explores our roots, the beliefs, values and sources of gratitude that anchor us to solid ground and stabilize us when the storms come. If our North point gives us a sense of direction (the *why* of our leadership), the South point explains our *how*.

We look at our Relationships in Chapter 6. Here we work through the three relationships that matter most when we are navigating our way through thin space:

our relationships with our secure bases, with our organization and with ourselves.

Finally, in Chapter 7 we look at the wise narrative of our resources, or the gifts we bring onto the stage of our leadership. Think of your resources as your skills and talents, but also as the character strengths that enable you to persist in the face of complexity and confusion.

As we will see in the next chapters, the point of our narrative work isn't just to have wise narratives in each compass point. It is also to ensure that all four points work in harmony. We'll explore how to establish this harmony, and what can get in the way of it, in the stories ahead.

PART TWO

THE LEADER'S COMPASS

CHAPTER 4

ORIENTATION (NORTH)

THE WISE NARRATIVE OF PURPOSE AND MEANING IN YOUR LIFE AND IN YOUR LEADERSHIP

Existential psychology has shown the depth of the human need to matter, make a difference, and feel a significant purpose in this world. We all need to feel that we do something that matters within the frame of reference that defines our experiential world. The question is, what is this frame of reference?

- CARLO STRENGER,
THE FEAR OF INSIGNIFICANCE

If your Leader's Compass is your ultimate inner ordering mechanism, the North point – your *Orientation* – is the part of the compass that plants your feet firmly on the ground and turns you in the right direction. Your Orientation is your calling, your purpose, the point of you in your life and in your leadership, the impact you want to have, the difference you want to make that calls you forward with a power that makes the hard work and difficulty along the way worth it.

You might think of your Orientation as your passion, since your passions are the things in your life that are important enough to justify the energy or pain required to realize them. You might also see it as the deepest longings of your soul, a definition that fits well, as we will see, with analytical psychology's belief that our purpose in the second half of our lives is the discovery and expression of our truest selves, those dimensions of us that we've hidden while we've taken on the task of conventional success. Your Orientation is your quest, to the extent that your life and your leadership are in pursuit of something good. It is your lasting impact, the legacy that makes your journey a good one. We all operate according to a sense of Orientation but, as we will also see, we often settle for an unconscious Orientation that is not really our own.

In this chapter, we will look at Orientation from the perspectives of our different clinical practices. I start with Orientation because of its extraordinary importance to our sense of psychological stability, resilience and understanding of ourselves. I also start with Orientation because it is the compass point to which the other compass points must harmonize. Our work is designed to create wise narratives in three aspects of your Orientation:

1. The story of the difference you want to make through your leadership, beyond the usual key performance indicators.
2. The story of your leadership from the elephant's perspective.
3. The story of how you define success in your life and in your leadership.

WHAT CALLS YOU FORWARD

When post-traumatic growth researchers write about the importance of the wise narrative of our purpose, they are capturing an observation that is shared across almost all schools of clinical psychology. That observation is that *we are more psychologically grounded when we live our lives with a conscious sense of purpose.*

Each of our five schools of psychology has its own point of view about why our Orientation is so critical. According to the existentialists, purpose is what gives a feeling of significance to our lives. It enables us to face our anxieties about death, isolation, freedom and meaninglessness honestly. Psychologist and holocaust survivor Viktor Frankl famously launched a school of psychology built on his observation that the concentration camp prisoners who were most likely to survive their experiences psychologically and physically intact were those who felt they had a transcendent meaning or significance in their lives. Frankl writes: "I admonish my students: 'Don't aim at success – the more you aim at it and make it a target, the more you are going to miss it. For success, like happiness, cannot be pursued; it must ensue, and it only does so as the unintended side effect of one's personal dedication to a cause greater than oneself.'"[42] By a 'cause greater than oneself,' Frankl refers to Orientation.

Evolutionary psychology describes survival and nurturing the next generation as our deepest purpose, embedded in our psychological DNA because without it we would have lost our species' survival battle long ago. Analytical psychology picks up where evolutionary psychology ends. It says that while evolution may explain all the compromises we make in the first half of life – the part of our lives that we dedicate to conventional success, establishing a secure life, starting and raising a family – thanks to our greatly expanded lifespans, we now have to deal with a second half of life for which evolution doesn't provide a program. In the absence of evolutionary programming, it says, our purpose in the second half of our lives is to become our true selves, living with higher integrity to the essence of what is truly important to us. The psychologist Eric Erikson provides some detail into how our sense of purpose changes as we age. He identified eight stages of development, each of which comes with its own conflict. Our purpose at each stage is to successfully resolve that stage's conflict. For leaders, Erikson's description of the conflict between Generativity vs Stagnation, the seventh stage (typically between 40–65 years old) is especially important. During this stage, we are driven to contribute to the development of the world through our families, our communities and our work. If we fail at this task, we suffer from a sense of insignificance and isolation.[43]

Even our religions reflect an innate wisdom that we are guided best when we are guided to serve a purpose, and that this purpose shifts as we progress through different stages of our life. In his description of Hinduism, for example, Huston Smith describes its emphasis on acting in ways that are appropriate to our stage in life. Hinduism teaches about the stage of the student (life's first stage), which is followed by a second stage dedicated to attending to family, vocation and civic participation. According to Huston:

> Hinduism smiles on the happy fulfilment of these wants but does not try to prime them when they begin to ebb. That attachment to them should eventually decline is altogether appropriate, for it would be unnatural for life to end while action and desire are at their zenith. If we follow the seasons as they come, we shall notice a time when sex and the delights of the senses (pleasure), as well as achievement in the game of life (success), no longer yield novel and surprising turns; when even the responsible discharge of human vocation (duty) begins to pall, having grown repetitive and stale. When this season arrives, it is time for the individual to move on to the third stage in life's sequence.[44]

The third of life's four stages, the stage of the hermit, is devoted to service and the pursuit of deriving wisdom from life's many lessons.

WHAT HAPPENS WHEN WE LOSE OUR ORIENTATION

One indication of the central importance of our sense of Orientation is what happens to us when we are without one, or at least without one that feels authentic to us.

The best way to describe the confusion that settled into Ash, me and many of the executives whom I work with is that we became disoriented when we lost a convincing answer to the question: *What is the point of my work?*

Ash was driven by a desire to protect the safety of her organization's customers and safeguard her organization's reputation. That Orientation disappeared when Ash felt that her work was being ignored. Although I didn't have a conscious sense of purpose during my own experience, my unconscious purpose would have been something like "to help my organization become the best in the world at helping leaders become more resilient, more able to withstand the inevitable storms of leadership, and more able to shape their organizations for the better." A less-admirable addition would have been to enhance my sense of personal capability, my status and my financial situation. I lost all of that when I understood that my purpose wasn't aligned with the organization.

It was a lonely feeling. We can feel lost when we don't know where we want to go. Without my Orientation, I struggled to find answers to basic questions: *If I'm not doing what I'm doing now, what should I do? If not working where I am working now, where should I be working? If I am not who I used to be, who do I want to become?* It's a difficult thing to feel abandoned by people you've trusted. It's just as difficult to feel betrayed by an Orientation that doesn't work any more. It is even more daunting when you open yourself up to the suspicion that the beautiful purpose you've dedicated tremendous time and effort to serving isn't so beautiful.

One danger of living without a wise narrative of our Orientation is that we adapt someone else's by default. It can be frightening to search for a path that fits with what is most important to us, especially when the obvious 'first half of life' answers to the question of our purpose – to be conventionally successful, raise a family, become financially secure – are all taken care of. Organizations provide easy substitutes. But if we frame our Orientation in terms of how we can be the best instrument of the organization's short-term financial success, we leave ourselves vulnerable to dismay and discomfort when poor results come for reasons that are beyond our control.

WHAT IT IS, AND WHAT IT ISN'T

Developing a sense of Orientation that is wise enough to be useful takes serious work, but before we get to the work, let's make sure we understand what Orientation is, and what it isn't. Let's start with what it isn't.

Orientation is not a goal whose only value is found in a reward you will receive once it's been achieved. Orientation is its own reward. If I think that my purpose is to get the next big promotion because it comes with a healthy raise, I'm focused on the result. I am not thinking of the intrinsic importance of the impact I will make along the way. You might argue that financial reward is helpful because it means I can secure a better life for my kids, in which case it's more useful to think of the result rather than the means by which you achieve the result. Thinking only of the reward risks losing our focus on the impact that is most meaningful to us. For example, I can convince myself that I want that big promotion because of the raise it brings and what the extra money means for how I can take care of my family. However, it might also be that the reward is attractive for less purposeful reasons: to stroke my ego; as a number I can use to compare myself favourably to others or evaluate my worth; as an indication of my status or as an imagined step up in my life that might calm the persistent voice inside of me that tells me that I am not good enough. Thinking about the ultimate impact I want to have – raising a healthy and well-adjusted family, for example – might mean I have certain financial targets in mind. But it also leaves the door open to the many nonfinancial ways I can act as a secure base to my family, by sharing my time, guidance and whatever wisdom I've earned along the ups and downs of my life.

A wise Orientation is not a guarantee that life will be smooth and seamless. It is not a panacea for whatever ills may come your way. Orientation doesn't mean that you avoid life's storms. It doesn't mean that you'll never get confused about the right thing to do when you seem to have only bad choices. It isn't a statement that brings you everlasting peace or infuses you with joy whenever you think of it.

And, finally, Orientation isn't set in stone. It isn't the one thing you can rely on to guide you throughout your entire adult life. As we've seen, our sense of Orientation shifts as we pass through life's different stages. While it's true that many of our most important shifts have taken place by the time we reach a senior leadership role, it's also true that we have plenty of time to explore different Orientations even after we've reached a high level of career success. We work with many CEOs who want to explore the possibility that their move to the highest level of leadership in their organization is more meaningful than the stress it brings or the financial rewards that come with it. Money typically isn't an issue for them, and their families are usually mature enough to have found at least some stability. In most cases, our CEOs aren't searching for conventional definitions of success. They are searching for an understanding of how their new leadership territory can bring deeper levels of meaning to their lives.

If our Orientation isn't a permanent anchor, or a guarantee of happiness, or a path to some other reward, what is it? I can best share the answer to that question through a personal story.

After I left my old organization, I had a difficult time sorting out what to do with my career. I had a good 15 or 20 years of work ahead of me. I hadn't yet made sense of what had gone so wrong in my old role. I felt betrayed by a purpose that had failed me when I needed it the most. And I wasn't quite sure what I wanted to do next. My old expertise wasn't interesting enough to encourage me forward: the last thing I wanted after the previous chapter of my life was to keep doing the same old work. I wasn't interested in *more*. I was interested in *different*. I just wasn't sure what *different* meant.

I explored different possibilities without much sense of how to evaluate them. I thought about taking whatever reasonable job came first, although something in me told me that there was danger in turning toward safety rather than exploration. I was financially secure enough to keep my family going for a little while. So, I explored. I thought about developing the credentials to bring myself to the level of the people who had caused me so much trouble in my previous role, but I understood quickly that there was too high a cost to pay to arm myself for a war that I'd already lost. I thought about a corporate role, but wondered if such a role would give me the freedom to experiment and, especially, control the circumstances of my work. I thought about joining another consultancy but was at a loss to understand how to differentiate between them. After some reflection, I understood that my challenge wasn't just deciding what to do next. My challenge was sorting out which criteria I could trust to guide me to wise choices.

At the time, I was on a couple of industry association boards. During a conversation with one of my board colleagues about possibilities for my future, he mentioned that I might want to take some time to identify my 'purpose.' Organizational purpose work was becoming popular at the time, and I'd heard about some religious leader in the United States writing a book about a purpose-driven life, but I was skeptical that I could sort out a wise direction for my life through some generic process. I was suspicious of simple answers to what I saw as complex psychological challenges. I imagined some pseudo-academic promising a path to purpose through five easy steps, or some similar sugar. I felt I needed something deeper and more grounded in who I was and who I wanted to be. I was jaded by so many of the consultants and academics I'd come across in my long career in leadership development who seemed to sell slick solutions to deeply profound challenges. By that time, I'd developed a severe allergy to slickness.

Nevertheless, I put myself through a three-day purpose workshop designed and delivered by a credible group that some friends had recommended to me. I remember being ill at ease and a little lost during the workshop. I wasn't at my best in those days, and my sense of confusion sometimes bled over into my social and professional interactions.[45] We were all strangers in the room, something like 20 of us, and over three days we worked together to try to understand ourselves better. We looked at our values, at the moments in our lives when we felt at our best, at when we felt most offended or repulsed by what we witnessed at work or in our lives.

At the end of the three days, we were each asked to share with the rest of the group what we had crafted as our purpose statement over the course of our time together. The purpose statement was meant to be an integration of all our explorations into who were, who we wanted to be, what meant the most to us in our lives. It was meant to have certain set ingredients to it, a certain established format. For the life of me, no matter how hard I tried, I couldn't construct one that felt in the least bit meaningful.

As much as I scribbled away, whatever I wrote felt incomplete. I wrote the sentences of someone who was trying to answer the test correctly rather than of someone who had a profound realization to share. I understand now that my writing was rider writing. My discomfort was my elephant telling me that it had a story to tell.

Shortly before it was my turn to step in front of the group to share my purpose statement, my elephant came to the rescue.

For some reason, I started to think about some of the most meaningful times in my life. My mind wandered to the camping trips I used to take to Algonquin Park, a huge land of lakes, rivers and forest only a few hours' drive from our family home in Ottawa. My best vacations were taken in that land, sometimes with my father, sometimes with friends and other family members. I remembered how on edge I felt sometimes in Algonquin, where most of the protections of civilization fall behind and we're no longer on top of the food chain. I remembered how much I felt 'in between' there. I remembered also a movie about exploring the Canadian wilderness by canoe that a local artist and filmmaker named Bill Mason had once filmed about his years canoe-camping in the Great Lakes. He called his movie *Waterwalker.* He explained that the title was a metaphor for what it means to travel by canoe over Canada's rivers and lakes. But he was a man of faith as well, and he explained that the idea of water-walking also had an important spiritual meaning for him.

Suddenly I had my answer. When I stood in front of the group, I told them simply: my purpose is to help people walk on water. I explained the cultural and religious meaning behind the metaphor. I told a story from the New Testament – the same story that Bill Mason, the canoeist and movie producer, told in his film about what it means to walk on water. I am not conventionally religious, but I went to Catholic schools when I grew up and became familiar with and fascinated by biblical narratives. I told the group that there's a story in the New Testament of how the followers of Jesus took a boat out onto the Sea of Galilee, while Jesus rested onshore. The wind was ferocious, and all the boat's passengers began to fear for their lives. Suddenly, Christ walked toward them over the water, safe and sound and unafraid, standing calmly atop the waves. From out in the storm's chaos, Christ beckons to Peter, one of his most important followers, to come walk to him. Peter does, successfully for a few steps, until he realizes what he's doing. Then he remembers that he shouldn't be able to do what he is doing, and he sinks into the waves.

I told the group that I wanted to help leaders to rise above their storms. To use their difficulties understand themselves better. To grow. To develop toward their wisest selves. To be safe in their knowledge of who they are. To help them teach others to be safe as well. I was working hard to survive my own storm. I wanted to use what I was learning to help others survive theirs.

I didn't really know what I meant – the image that my unconscious mind conjured up was right, it felt right, but it was packed with meaning that I hadn't yet explored. I knew that my story didn't fit the conventional structure that the facilitators had suggested for a good purpose statement. Over the coming months, I tried to understand the metaphor and what it might be telling me. I knew that I'd identified a problem that had captured my imagination, that sat deep within me. I knew that I felt strongly about how carelessly organizations often treat their leaders, how they promote smart and enthusiastic people into highly chaotic roles and leave them without the support they need and deserve. I knew that we – the organizations themselves and the consultancies and business schools that claim to want to help them – were failing badly. I knew I had some nascent points of view about why we were failing, and what we might do to help leaders avoid their own failures.

I came to understand two things about my Orientation metaphor. First, that the spirit of the story contained a powerful sense of purpose for me. It captured my imagination and with it my energy and determination. And second, that to honour this sense of purpose I had a lot of hard work ahead of me.

I also came to understand that having my Orientation in my mind and in my heart helped me through some important personal and professional challenges. I'll list the ways it helped me here so that you have a sense of my relationship with my Orientation, but the list isn't all-inclusive. Everyone's wise Orientation narrative is different. Everyone's Orientation metaphor is packed with its own levels of meaning, its own hints and shadows. Each Orientation will help its author according to the needs of the author's own journey.

Developing the wise story of my Orientation helped me in four ways:

1. *It showed me the way out of chaos.* All the loud confusion that came from my leadership battles about who I was, who I wanted to be, what I wanted to do now that I wasn't in my old job any more, was calmed by the image of my Orientation. When these questions came up, I had a satisfying answer. With the image of water-walking in my imagination, I knew that I wanted to do *that*. Orientation gave me a clear enough sense of my forward direction that I could start to feel drawn toward the future rather than attached to a painful past.

2. *It helped me make choices.* My Orientation gave me a set of criteria that enabled me to start making wise choices about what to do next. Whatever choices felt coherent with achieving my sense of Orientation felt right. Choices that turned me away from it felt wrong. With my metaphor in mind, I was able to pivot the topic of my doctoral research, choose an organization that would help me to explore what water-walking work looked like and would enable me to build the skills that I needed to become more helpful to the leaders I wanted to help. For me, Orientation was not just a call forward. It was also an organizing principle.

3. *It moved me toward growth.* Crafting my Orientation was a pivotal step for me in being able to work intentionally with my narrative world rather than to be a victim of intrusive narrative thinking. Remember that in post-traumatic growth work, the path to wiser narratives is the single most important step toward growth. Remember, as well, that the turn toward wiser narratives is a turn away from intrusive rumination and toward intentional rumination. In positive psychology framing, it is also the turn away from protective negative emotion (fear, anger, hatred, anxiety) toward positive, generative emotion (joy, hope, optimism). My Orientation metaphor was a happy metaphor for me. It showed me a hopeful, meaningful future.

4. *It gave me a frame in which I could explore what it means to be a leader.* Framing leadership in terms of water-walking gave me a host of images to play with when I explored leadership: images of difficult storms, violent undercurrents, dark and deep waters, but also images of rising above, of being lifted and pulled forward by a sense of your highest self, of using storms as ways to

test who you are and who you want to be. All of these images were material that I was able to explore in my doctoral work. In an important way the frame of my Orientation gave me a unique way to imagine what leadership really is, especially in terms of the many opportunities for profound growth that it can give us. The frame was a request from my elephant that I look at myself, my purpose in my work and in my life in a way that honoured what was most important to me.

TRAPS AND TIPS

We face important hurdles when we turn our attention toward our Orientation. If we put our rider in charge of the exercise, we can find ourselves searching for dry answers to fertile questions. If we settle for the obvious, we let what's efficient blind us to what's meaningful. If we rely too much on what we've been told and what we've been taught, we end up following someone else's path.[46]

In our Orientation work, there are three steps that help us jump over these hurdles:

1. **Start with your rider**
    We're used to letting the rider lead the way in our leadership work, and so it's helpful to let the rider start the process. Think about times when you felt at your very best, when you were making the kind of difference you like to make. Think about when you received praise that touched you in a particularly deep way, or when you finished a challenge that held a deeper meaning than the reward you might have received upon completing it.

If you're heading into a role transition, imagine yourself a year into the future, receiving the praise you'd like to receive for making the kind of difference that you would like to have made. If you're undertaking a more significant transition – say, into the final chapter of your career – think about what you would like people to thank you for when you hold a retirement party for all the people whom you've touched and who've touched you during your career. Distill all of this down to a few sparse sentences – think Hemingway, not Foucault – so that the essence of your Orientation is captured as simply as possible. My rider's version of my Orientation back at the time of my career change was captured in the sentences I wrote above: I wanted to help organizations prepare their leaders for their most difficult challenges, grow because of these challenges rather than be destroyed by them, and use their strength and stability to step into the hard work of demanding more and better from the organizations in which they lead. I might have summarized my rider's description as: *I help leaders become stronger and deeper so that they can make their organizations better.* Other summary examples from recent Orientation work include:

I reach into crisis and make order out of it.

I solve the problems that no one else in the organization dares to solve.

I make us all better, one small step at a time.

I develop our organization and our people so that together we can proudly contribute to a better industry and a better world.

I disrupt so that we never stagnate and so that we are always searching for a better version of ourselves.

Notice three things about the examples above. First, they are simple. They capture an essential idea without distracting away from it with too much unnecessary colour. Second, they are vague enough to cover wide territory, although to the author of each Orientation statement, they are a useful first step into identifying the territory they want to explore. Third, they are oriented toward action. They are calls to movement rather than reflection. They each demand effort on behalf of the author.

2. **Dig deep**
   You might have struggled to come to find a satisfying answer in step one. Your struggle could be because your rider recognizes that we are all driven by multiple purposes, that sometimes these purposes run in parallel and sometimes they are replaced as we step into new stages in our lives. I hinted at this complexity when I mentioned that while I wanted to help leaders become strong enough to change their organizations for the better, I also wanted a job that enabled me to take care of my family. Here we get to an important challenge. Our Orientation must be both achievable and aspirational. It must reflect where we are in our journey through life, and yet draw us forward to the next stages as well. This challenge is particularly confusing when we are working our way through a difficult transition and feel ourselves pulled toward security and away from creativity. It explains why Orientation work is sometimes clearer for senior executives who are advanced in their careers and who've already checked the box of financial security. A good Orientation recognizes what's essential and integrates what calls us forward.

It doesn't sacrifice what calls us forward for what's purely pragmatic. It doesn't sacrifice what's pragmatic for an unachievable dream.

A good way to test if your initial Orientation statement hits the right mark is to push yourself toward deeper possibilities. If your rider's initial reaction to the question of Orientation is something like *"To make more money so that I can secure my family"* or *"To achieve higher status in the hierarchy,"* your rider might be rightfully focusing on an outcome that's fundamental to your stage in life. Accept the guidance. But ask it: *"And then what?"* Once you've achieved that goal, what's the next level of meaning for your leadership? You might answer *"To achieve strong results"* in whatever project, business or function that falls under your leadership. Perfect. Accept that guidance too. Ask again: *"And then what?"* The question might turn you toward a broader circle of influence, away from the personal toward the team you lead or the organization your leadership serves. You might answer: *"To help my team become a more resilient source of ideas and innovation"* or *"To help develop leaders of tomorrow that are even wiser and stronger than our leaders of today."* With this third step, we are stepping toward a deeper legacy. A wise Orientation tends to look beyond what is close, toward the kinds of long-lasting systemic impact we want to have through our leadership.

3. **Let your elephant speak**
   Finally, and critically, after you've played with what might be a rational sense of your Orientation and peeled back a few layers of meaning in your work with it, invite your elephant into the conversation. Inviting your elephant in means asking it to identify a story, metaphor, image, symbol or figure that best represents the spirit

of your Orientation. My elephant served me with the multifaceted image of water-walking. I could see in my image the positive, radiant image of the higher self, calling out to a struggling figure sinking into the stormy waves, struggling to stay afloat. I am not anyone in the image: rather, I am the spirit of the image. I am the force that encourages leaders to imagine that higher version of themselves that supports them and calls them forward, above the waves and into a way of being in which storms don't matter. I continue to take meaning out of the metaphor – even writing about it in this chapter has helped me understand what the Christ figure really means in my metaphor. That's what our elephants do. They provide us with guidance in their metaphorical language.

A strange thing happens when I encourage leaders to think of a story, a character or a metaphor that captures the essence of who they are when they are making the difference they want to make. I offer them the challenge. They hesitate, often look aimlessly into the air for a few seconds, and then they say something like "*Nothing comes to mind right away.*" I leave an awkward silence between us for a few seconds, after which the leader invariably says, "*Actually, now that you ask, something does come to mind.*" The sequence of hesitation-then-realization points to an interesting inner mechanism that shows how our riders and elephants sometimes dance together. "*Nothing comes to mind*" is the rider saying that he doesn't really understand the question. Myths and metaphors aren't his territory. The few seconds of awkward hesitation are the time it takes for the rider to surrender the stage to the elephant, who is happy to step forward. Our cultures provide us with an enormous library of stories and characters from which our elephants can draw. Mine chose an old biblical tale that made sense to me because of my upbringing. Other leaders draw from fairy tales, movies and other cultural icons to articulate their Orientation. For example:

I am Captain America. I sit in the midst of the battle and calmly mobilize all of us according to each of our superpowers into the fight for a better world (referring to a leading but nuanced character in popular Marvel movies).

I am the enchantress who turns pumpkins into carriages (referring to a childhood fairy tale).

I am a little less Roger Federer and a little more Trevor Noah, engaging people in the narrative of what's good through a mix of stable order and playful chaos (referring to a recent advertisement here in Switzerland in which two Swiss-South African celebrities, one an athlete and one a comedian, play off their distinctive personalities to market the idea of vacationing in Switzerland).

I am Fred the Penguin: I convince people that unless we change our ways, our ice will melt and we will be in big trouble (referring to an old John Kotter book titled *Our Iceberg Is Melting* on how to convince the resistant people around you to change even though change is difficult).

These are only a few examples of how the elephant speaks when it's invited into the territory of Orientation. Sometimes our initial Orientation thoughts resonate immediately with our elephant. Sometimes they need greater exploration before they fully settle into us. The important task is to make sure the elephant stays on our stage as we explore the types of stories that capture the elephant's sense of what our meaningful Orientation might be.

SUMMARY

We rely on our sense of Orientation to guide us through life's complexities. Orientation keeps us headed in the right direction. It sets criteria for how we spend our time, how we make difficult decisions, the compromises we can and can't make. Our Orientation reflects the legacy we want to leave. If our leadership is a platform for making a difference, our Orientation describes the difference we want to make.

Our rider thinks about our Orientation in rational and measurable terms. The elephant conjures up its own metaphors, symbols and stories to convey a meaningful Orientation. It draws upon all the myths and legends our culture gives to us to identify a deeper sense of our Orientation than our rider can provide. The Orientation definitions that come from our rider and our elephant may sound different, but their spirit should be essentially the same so that our conscious and unconscious minds are headed in the same direction.

Like all our compass points, the wise narrative of our Orientation evolves over time. What might be a good Orientation at 25 won't be as useful when we reach 45 or 60. Also, like all our compass points, the narrative stays wise only if we change it to integrate new experiences and new desires. Leadership transitions are useful opportunities for updating our Orientation so that we can be sure it calls us forward in our new context.

1. When was the last time someone thanked you for something and you were deeply touched by their expression of gratitude? What did they thank you for? Why were you touched by it? Describe the difference you made in that person's life in as much detail as you can.

2. Imagine that you are a few years in the future and you have finished the current chapter of your leadership story. It has been a tremendous success. You have achieved all that you wanted to achieved, and you are ready to turn to your next adventure. But before you do, you decide to throw a celebration with all the people you've touched, and who have touched you, over the previous years. You invite colleagues, perhaps people on your team and some of the people who report to them, mentors, friends, family. You invite anyone and everyone who has been important to you over these years, and many of the people that you have been important to as well.

   You've chosen a wonderful place to hold your event, and over the meal you notice the energy around the room. People are chatting, laughing, sharing stories. But soon dinner is winding down, dessert and coffees are being served, and the music is getting a little bit quieter and the lighting a little softer. No one is leaving, but you notice that people are beginning to mingle around the room, in small groups of two or three. You decide to take the opportunity to wander around to these small groups to say hello. As you go from group to group, each person you approach takes the opportunity of your little moment of intimacy to thank you for the difference you have made to them over the previous years.

Who is there, and what would you like them to thank you for?

CHAPTER 5

ROOTS (SOUTH)

THE WISE NARRATIVE OF YOUR CORE BELIEFS AND ESSENTIAL VALUES

*Life is good when you live
from your roots. Your values
are a critical source of energy,
enthusiasm and direction.
Work is meaningful and fun
when it's an expression
of your true core.*

- SHOSHANA ZUBOFF

Across from Orientation and at the compass's South point are our Roots. Our Roots are our core narratives about who we are and about how we believe we should operate in the world. They include our core values and our most important beliefs. They also include the way we think about what it means to lead a good life. Our Roots settle deep below the surface and guide us, often without our awareness. We have a healthy Root system when we know what we really believe and truly value because we've tested our beliefs and values against our experience.

Post-traumatic growth gives our Root system special attention. Researchers in the field observe that growth, even through the most chaotic experience, often takes the form of what they call 'a changed philosophy of life.' The term encompasses the sense of life's purpose that we covered in the previous chapter. It also encompasses our beliefs about life and about ourselves, as well as the ways in which we prioritize our time. In the researchers' words: [47]

The (traumatized) person may experience increased satisfaction in playing with a toddler, being more deeply touched by a beautiful sunset or simply relishing the delight of spending time with warm and close friends.

American veterans who experienced the brutal conditions in POW camps, for example, may report how they still relish the simple pleasure of eating a hot dog or licking an ice cream cone.

An encounter with a traumatic event can provide a strong lesson that much of what we love is temporary, so we should deliberately engage with the most important parts of our lives while we can.

Many of the survivors of a ship that sank some years ago reported that they no longer took life for granted, and three out of four indicated that they now made it a priority to live each day to the fullest.

For some people, the encounter with trauma can make salient, as never before, that everyday experiences and relationships are important, and maybe should be given a higher priority.[48]

In life and in leadership, post-transitions growth often comes through the exploration and reconstruction of what we believe about ourselves, how the world works, and what we value in our lives. The wise narrative of our values and beliefs gives us a Root system that is healthy enough to keep us secure in the face of the inevitable storms of life and leadership. Developing the wise narratives of our Roots entails an exploration of how we spend our time, what we value in our lives, and from where we derive our greatest satisfaction and fulfilment.

Our Roots sit at the opposite end of our Leader's Compass because there is an important connection between the two. While our Orientation calls us forward to what is new, our Roots give us stability. Their solidity and strength help us navigate through our daily lives with confidence. They enable us to withstand the normal storms of living without being toppled over. They are the maps that we have formed, through evolution and through our many years of wisdom-giving experience, so that we can walk through the territory of life without questioning every step. As we shall see, however, the wise narrative of our Orientation asks us to re-examine our values and beliefs to make sure that old, inherited beliefs aren't holding us back from living the way our Orientation calls us to live.

Exploring our Roots means exploring three different territories:

1. The beliefs and values that guide us, especially when we are under threat.
2. Our definition of a successful life.

3. The activities that give us the greatest sense of renewal and positive emotion (peace, joy, happiness, optimism, hope, love).

Before we get to the exploration of the three territories, I'll share a few words about why it's important to dig into both our conscious and unconscious responses to them.

Remember that most of what is chaotic and mysterious about us sits in the territory of our elephant, and most of what gives us a sense of order in our lives sits in the territory of our rider. Since our sense of who we are is an important ordering mechanism for us, the rider likes to believe that they understand the territory best. This belief is evident when we ask leaders to list their most important values. The list usually contains the same words – trust, integrity, fairness, respect, to name a few common values that tend to sit on top of our values hierarchy. It's only when we start digging into elephant territory that we begin to understand how influential certain values and beliefs are, and to discern whether or not they have outlived their usefulness. It's also important to refer back to my comments in previous chapters (and again referenced at the beginning of this chapter) that the parts of us that contribute most strongly to our sense of identity are likely to be the things in us that resist change most stubbornly. The clinical observation is that we tend to change our most important values and beliefs only when a crisis forces us to. But if we ask our rider and our elephant to explore together, we can evolve our Root systems without the stress of a major crisis.

Taking an example from my own leadership, I remember three unconscious beliefs that served me well over the years. Each of these beliefs was invalidated during my leadership transition, but each of them resisted my attempts to leave them behind. The three beliefs were:

- The more I commit to the organization I serve, the more it will commit to me.
- The best strategy for career success is to keep my head down and do good work.
- I'll be able to resolve all my important work conflicts with smart diplomacy.

They seemed like wise beliefs. For most of my career, they worked. Operating according to these beliefs helped me earn years of positive performance reviews and healthy bonuses. There were some downsides: for example, I was annoyed when colleagues were rewarded because of the relationships they nurtured rather than for their contribution to the organization's success. And I wasn't thrilled when one of my bosses praised me because he thought I was able to 'take a lot of crap' without getting bothered by it. 'Crap-taker' wasn't high on the list of adjectives that I wanted associated with my name. But I brushed off these annoyances by telling myself that my beliefs were wise, and that you can call wisdom whatever you want, it's still wisdom.

Positive reviews and healthy bonuses encouraged me to stick with my beliefs. I did, and they worked, until suddenly they didn't. My transition proved that they were insufficient. Sometimes, when leadership is weak and wants to please powerful but badly-behaved colleagues, the organization doesn't love you back. Sometimes putting your head down and focusing on the work just makes you an easy target for people who want to sabotage you. Sometimes appealing to the best in other people doesn't work because their best is buried beneath their ambition. When people act like monsters, sometimes it's useful to show them that you can be a monster too.

I hated giving up on my three beliefs. I held them closely, almost desperately, even when my experience was telling me that they didn't work. Letting them go felt like letting go of what made me a good person. I noticed that my rider wasn't very useful in this strange territory of unwise beliefs, and so I asked my elephant to join the struggle. I eventually asked him some of the questions that we will turn to next: *What part of me clings to these beliefs? Where do they come from, and what do they represent to me? What would I lose if I modified these beliefs so that they reflected what I now know to be true?* As usual with elephant work, I tried to communicate through images and metaphors and symbols. And, as usual, my elephant served up to me a useful image in response. The image was of a scared child who clung to some old beliefs as if they were branches hanging over a rushing river. The child didn't want to let go of the branch because letting go meant being taken away by the river's rushing current. My elephant also served to me an image of a calmer, wiser me who was quite happy to let go, knowing that the river was just a river, that I'd travelled down many rivers before, and that adjusting my narratives about these three beliefs would make me a better river-traveller.

With help from my elephant, a wiser version of each belief emerged:

"The more I commit to the organization I serve, the more it will commit itself to me" became "Care for it as much as you like but don't treat an organization as if it's there to make you happy. Care for yourself and protect yourself too."

"I'll succeed if I keep my head down and do good work" became "Everyone brings their elephants to work with them and sometimes those elephants behave badly. Good work and results matter, but so does paying attention to the herd of elephants that show up to your workplace every single day."

"Smart diplomacy will resolve my work challenges" became "Every so often someone will want to get you out of the way. Make sure these people know that there are significant costs to taking you on."

Leaders at all levels often suffer from the consequences of outdated Root systems. It's understandable. The work is challenging, and leaders typically have many other tasks on their plate. We use our three territories to help us structure our exploration.

THE CORE BELIEFS AND ESSENTIAL VALUES THAT GUIDE US, ESPECIALLY WHEN WE ARE THREATENED

Our first territory asks us to examine the beliefs and values that form the core of our Root system. It may seem like a gentle start, but we face a series of challenges when we turn our attention in this direction.

An initial challenge is that it is difficult to arrange our values into a hierarchy. It's not always obvious which values we would never want to compromise, which are important but can be compromised given the right benefits, and which are useful but not so important that we would give it much thought if we needed to compromise them for a greater good. Our values typically move up and down a hierarchy. There's a fluidity to them that allows us to move with agility in the face of life's demands. Sorting out what is essential, always, no matter what the circumstances, requires careful exploration.

Second, we tend to think about our values in terms of easy and shallow labels that prevent us from developing a deeper understanding of what they really are. Ask any group of leaders about what values drive them and you're likely to get a crowd of positive responses around easy labels: *trust, fairness, integrity, respect, collaboration.* These are important values. They are popular because they have been wired into us for their survival benefits. We like fairness because we are more comfortable playing the game when we know the rules and we know that they are applied equally. We like respect because humiliation is a powerful reminder of our vulnerability to those who are stronger than we are. We like integrity because we operate with greater confidence when we believe that everyone shares the same understanding of our standards of acceptable behaviour. Unfortunately, the labels don't do a good job of explaining exactly what they mean in the context of our leadership. We accept them as if we know what they mean, but we don't actually understand how these values influence us. And we don't know them well enough to understand what to do when important values come into conflict with each other, or when we find that our leadership work asks us to compromise something inside of us that doesn't want to be compromised.

Which leads to our third values challenge. If we don't know what our values really are and we don't really understand what we really mean, how can we begin to understand how these values operate in our Root system? How can we work with our values if we don't really know what material we are working with?

As always with exploration in elephant territory, it's best to dig beneath the surface. I've found several effective ways to dig. Each method frames what we mean by values in a slightly different way. Two examples are:

THINK ABOUT THE LAST TIME YOU WERE SO ANGRY, SCARED OR WORRIED THAT YOU STRUGGLED TO CONTROL YOUR EMOTIONS.

Now think about why the emotions showed up. There's a wonderful saying from Carl Jung, founder of analytical psychology: *where your fear is, there is your task.* He means: where your emotions are highest, there is the territory for exploration. I was angriest when I felt I was being mistreated by people who wanted to game the organization's rules for their personal benefit. I was also angriest when people I believed were friends declined to support me. I was most anxious when I felt I was having to fight a battle in which my opponents could fight however they wanted, while I had both hands tied behind my back. I was most afraid when I felt that I was destined to fail because the organizational system was rigged against me. When I started to dig into what these emotions were trying to tell me, I began to understand some of their messages.

My anger was telling me that I placed a huge value on working together for the benefit of the organization, and that I needed to understand the limitations of this value in the context of leadership. It was also telling me that I had placed just as much value on the idea of friendship and human connection in the workplace, and that this value needed a similar reflection.

My anxiety was telling me that I valued fairness. I began to understand that if I wanted fairness so much, I needed to either find a different place to work or to find a way to make the cost of unfairness against me too high for the people who wanted to treat me unfairly to bear.

My fear was telling me that I valued being a good provider to the people I love, that I valued being seen as successful, that I valued being seen as a good leader. My fear was also telling me that it might be time to think carefully about the price I was paying to check all of those boxes. It was telling me that the price might be too high, and that my definitions of success might be too focused on what other people thought of me rather than what I thought of myself.

All of these emotions were pointing me to the ways in which old values were becoming outdated, were in conflict with one another, or were in conflict with what I was being asked to do as a leader. Understanding the narrative that lay beneath my emotions helped me develop a clearer picture of the values work I needed to do.

THINK OF THE ORIENTATION IMAGE OR METAPHOR THAT YOUR ELEPHANT PROVIDED TO YOU IN THE LAST CHAPTER. WHAT VALUES MATTER MOST TO THAT CHARACTER OR IN THAT STORY?

This second approach engages your elephant directly in your values work. Our elephants tend to provide us with images and metaphors that are packed with levels of deeper meaning, including messages about what really matters most for us. So, think about whatever image or symbols your elephant communicated to you in the work we did in the last chapter. What matters most to that image or character is likely to be what matters most to you. My Orientation image, the water-walker metaphor that drew from cultural artifacts of my Catholic education and my love of the Canadian outdoors, told me that I cared a lot about helping leaders gain wisdom from their storms. It also told me that I did NOT value being in the spotlight of this work. My elephant's image placed me as an observer and facilitator of a process but not as its main subject. My elephant was telling me that the work had to be about the guidance I could give to others rather than for my own glory. Finally, my elephant's image hinted that I would need to develop a serious expertise in the territory of growing through life's storms, that I couldn't fake my way through the work by claiming academic expertise. I needed to go through the process myself before I could help others go through it. I valued depth of understanding rather than slickness.

Similar stories come from clients. The 'Fred the Penguin' image I mentioned in the last chapter communicated the value of persistence when you want to warn the people around you of the dangers ahead. The 'Captain America' image, the one in which the leader was in the centre of a group of superheroes directing them all on how they can best use their powers, showed a shy leader the importance of being in the spotlight, confident in his own power so that he could help direct others to use their powers in the best possible way. The young leader whose elephant provided a 'less Roger Federer, more Trevor Noah' image – meaning a little less correct and a little more playful deconstruction – learned that a quiet but important part of him valued being a trickster, and that sometimes change only happens when leaders bring a little chaos into the game.

Jung turned us toward our emotions when we search for what is swirling within the elephant. It's also useful to ask our elephants directly, turning toward the metaphors and images that they've provided us in our Orientation work. When we turn toward another essential part of our Root system, our beliefs, we face similar challenges. Like our values, our beliefs become most meaningful when we try to understand whatever deeper wisdom they might hold. And, as with our values, we've developed some approaches to exploring our beliefs so that our elephants and our riders can get involved. I'll share two practices here.

LIST THE BELIEFS THAT YOU THINK MATTER MOST TO HOW YOU LEAD. THEN THINK ABOUT WHAT YOU WOULD DO IF EACH OF THESE BELIEFS WAS INVALIDATED.

Here we explore how important certain beliefs are to our Root system. You might remember the list of beliefs that I had when I entered into my leadership transition. I used them to highlight how trauma research observed that we suffer most when experience shatters our beliefs about the world's benevolence, its rationality and our own self-worth. I also mentioned some belief systems that clients have explored – systems that relied on beliefs in the value of long experience, about dedication to the organization's health over personal glory, about good work and strong results being rewarded rather than punished. It's useful to understand which of our beliefs are so essential to our Root system that we struggle to understand how we would cope if they were invalidated. The beliefs that resist invalidation most stubbornly are the beliefs that matter the most to our sense of who we are and how we should operate in the world.

The experiment looks like this. List all the beliefs that you believe are important to you in your leadership. These might be beliefs about what behaviour is appropriate, how organizations should operate, who gets rewarded or punished, who gets promoted or demoted. Once you've listed these beliefs, write down the story of how you would react if you learned that each belief was proved to be false. For example, how would you react if your organization promoted badly behaved leaders, or punished good behaviour, or if you learned that your boss doesn't actually want you to succeed, or if your long history of dedication to your organization meant that you were labelled as 'old school' by some fresh and ambitious newcomers. When you describe how you would react, pay attention to which examples stir up the strongest emotional response. The stronger the emotional response, the more likely it is that the belief being explored is critical to your Root system, and the more important it is to understand the narrative underneath the belief. Where does it come from? Why is it important? Is it your belief or is it someone else's? How would you refine the belief to make it a little bit wiser?

The second practice focuses on identifying and exploring old beliefs that might be getting in your way. The practice is this: **Write down what your critical internal voice tells you about who you are.** Once you've written this down, ask yourself: what wisdom and foolishness can be found in these messages? The purpose of this practice is to do two things: to understand that our inner critic is both useful and silly, and to understand the true nature of that part of us that tells us that we are not enough. In both cases, we are exploring some of the nuanced tensions at play within our elephant.

In the second case, it's useful to explore the messages that our inner critic sends us. Some common themes emerge from our exploration of the inner critics of even the most senior leaders. By far the most common of them is *"I am not good enough."* The fascinating thing about this message, and the reason it can be so disturbing, is that it is both absolutely true and completely false. It is absolutely true that none of us is enough to manage our way out of life's inevitable and random catastrophes or, as we saw in the opening chapters, out of the inevitability of our death. No matter how successful we think we are, or clever, or special, or blessed, we are just as vulnerable as most people to all the things in life that can go wrong. Existentially, none of us is enough to avoid the end of life. Death's inevitability and all the unsettling uncertainty associated with it is the reason death is the first of existential psychology's four main anxieties. The voice inside of us telling us that we are not enough is reminding us of this truth, perhaps with the hope that the message will guide us to live life to its fullest because of its brevity and randomness.

But the voice is absolutely false when it comes to our ability to manage what it means to be a leader. The message *I am not enough* is a lie when it comes to our ability to learn, gain wisdom from our experiences, do our best to understand what matters most to us and live our lives in a way that makes the narrative of our time here on Earth a story that makes us proud. We are all more than enough to do all of that exploration and wisdom-gathering. In fact, our ability and desire to explore ourselves are just as programmed into us as is the critical voice that tells us we need to be careful and to do more to arm ourselves against life's dangers.

This brings us to the first case. Why do we have an inner critic at all? What's the purpose of having a voice that seems so tirelessly dedicated to diminishing us or to holding us back? From an evolutionary perspective, the answer is simple. The voice is there because it wants to protect us. It is the voice that sees more threats than really exist because it's better to be careful than to step into unknown territory without first looking for danger. It's the voice that tells us that we better not take on too much risk because each risk we take brings the possibility of injury. And, importantly, it is a voice that emerges in us when we are young and vulnerable, and it is a voice that stays with all the subtlety, nuance and wisdom of a four-year-old unless we work hard to make it wiser. This is where our practical work lies. It's useful to nurture a habit of noticing our four-year-old inner critic who wants to warn us of all the real and imagined dangers of the world, and to pivoting the conversation away from that critic to wiser sources within us. A good habit to foster is to ask the four-year-old voice what it would communicate to you if it were a wise and mature adult. An even better habit to foster is to ask your Orientation character or image how it would translate what the four-year-old voice is trying to tell you. Both habits help us shift the strident and fearful four-year-old voice that behaves as if we are still four years old to a voice that understands our wisdom and appreciates all that our experience has taught us.

THE SUCCESSFUL LIFE

We explore two aspects of our Roots when we explore what it means to be successful. We test whether our beliefs about a successful life are really ours, and we test if our sense of what it means to lead a successful life is appropriate given our stage in life. Our Orientation evolves as we age. So, too, should our definitions of success.

The question is a challenging one because the rider and the elephant typically have competing but half-developed points of view and it's interesting to hear how they compete for ownership of the answer. I remember once being asked to provide assessment feedback for a group of 12 managing directors who worked in the asset management arm of a global bank. I agreed because our work gave me enough space to get to know the executives beyond whatever data the assessments provided. I met with each of the executives individually so that I could understand each person, at least a little, before reviewing what the assessments might be telling us about their leadership.

When I asked the executives what was important to them in their lives, each of them responded with stories that were refreshingly human and appropriate for their ages. They talked openly about how they loved spending time with their partners and young children, how they enjoyed their vacations and weekends away in the mountains, how they were happily occupied with the house they were renovating or the new apartment they were about to move into. But when I asked them about how they think about success, almost all of them gave some version of the same response: *I will be successful when I make as much money as my boss's boss.* Ask executives about what is important to them, and their elephants have at least a little say in the response. Ask them about success and the rider often sinks into conventional thinking about hierarchies, advancement up a corporate ladder and money as a way of monitoring progress.

FORMING OUR OWN DEFINITIONS OF SUCCESS

The first thing we test when we explore personal definitions of success is the extent to which the definitions of success that matter most to us are really ours, or if we've adapted them to get along with people that we've felt the need to please. It's not an easy question to answer because an important part of success in any life is measured in the richness of our relationships. Our relationships matter, and any relationship requires a healthy dance of give and take.

To explore the territory, we ask a deeper question about authenticity and compromise: To what extent do our current definitions of success require us to sacrifice important parts of who we are or who we want to become? I mentioned earlier that an important pivot in my leadership transition was when I realized that the sacrifices that were being demanded of me were slowly poisoning me. Making them would have prevented me from being the person I wanted to be. As much as I valued meeting all the conventional success criteria that came with my old role, I understood my personal definition of success meant maintaining dignity, agency and a belief that the leadership under which I served should meet some minimal quality standards. Staying in a role in which none of these definitions were met meant starving essential parts of my self.

How do we start exploring our own definitions of success? **First, by remembering that it is a complex question that resists definitive answers.** Just as our Orientation work is done best when it searches for meaning below the surface, Roots work is most effective when it explores which of our Roots nurture us best and grow deepest. To explore depth, it's useful to use the same *"And then what?"* approach that we used in our Orientation work. To use the example of my banking clients, I might ask: Once you make as much money as your boss's boss, *then what?* We might uncover something about raising healthy kids or providing for the family. *"And then what?"* A little digging might get us to something about the importance of making a difference to the people around us. *"And then what?"* The exercise gets more difficult with each successive round, but it's a helpful way to get beyond the obvious.

Second, by asking our Orientation what it's telling us about success. Here we see the importance of harmony between our Orientation and Roots system. We might say that the simplest way to think about success is that we are most successful when we are living in harmony with our Orientation. We can test this harmony by asking ourselves how much of ourselves is dedicated to following our Orientation, and how much of us is working in some other direction. The more I was spending my time exercising my old skills rather than building the new ones that my Orientation was telling me I needed to build, the more I was working against my inner harmony. The more the 'Fred the Penguin' executive works on her creative persistence, the more she is working in harmony with her Orientation. The more my 'Captain America' client avoids the uncomfortable spotlight that's required for him to take on the role of 'superpower organizer,' the less he's living in harmony with his Orientation.

Third, by keeping the most important people in our lives in mind when we think about our success. It's useful to have a 'Success Board' in our imaginations when thinking through our definition of success. I can then explore the extent to which the people who know me, whom I appreciate and trust, might agree with my definitions of success. I learned this wisdom from a client who was facing a difficult career choice. When we worked through his options, he kept mentioning how important it was for him to be able to explain his choices to his kids so that they would be proud of him and could learn from him. He ended up making a difficult choice, but the right choice, because it was the only choice that didn't feel like a compromise that he couldn't explain honestly to his children and still feel good about himself.

I'll share the example of my own Success Board. These are the people I keep in mind when I think about whether I am living a successful life and doing successful work. Each board member comes at the question in slightly different ways, but they would all approach it wanting the best for me:

- My clients. If I'm not useful to them, then I'm missing the calling of my Orientation. I know I am on the right track when clients tell me that I've helped them understand themselves better.

- Rox and Antoine, my wife and stepson. I want them both to be proud of me and my work, and to learn from me as much as I learn from them. I know that I am doing well when they are both curious about my work and take something for themselves from it.
- My father, a curious inquirer. If he's interested in where my explorations are taking me, then I know the territory is worth exploring.
- Bill Fischer, an old colleague and a friend whose instinct for digging below the surface helps me to see things that would otherwise remain hidden. If Bill is examining my work through his own lenses and pushing me to go even deeper, then I know he sees value in it.
- John, my friend, whose aversion to bullshit reminds me to always follow depth no matter how seductive easy answers can be.

It's important to remember that the point of the work isn't to please each member of the Success Board. And we don't actually need to talk to each of these people when we're evaluating how well we're doing in our lives. The point is to try to examine our lives through their eyes to see how the parts of them we value most might think about how well we are staying true to definitions of success that should matter most to us.

Fourth, by remembering success happens in many different dimensions of our lives. We might decide that we would like to be successful with work, family, friends, our own growth, our health and fitness, and our spiritual lives. And it might be that we aren't quite sure how well we are doing in each dimension, or if we are sacrificing some dimensions to favour others. It's useful to decide which dimensions are important to you, to describe what success looks like in each dimension, and see where rebalancing might be necessary. When I was working my way through my leadership chaos, I focused almost everything on my work. This is a common reflex in the face of massively destabilizing leadership experiences. Our attention goes toward survival. If the experience lasts a long time, however, we forget that the people around us might be living their own dramas. I knew I had some changes to make when I forgot about an important doctor's appointment that my wife was going to regarding some disturbing and potentially dangerous symptoms she was experiencing. She was cleared by the doctor, but I knew that I'd become too self-sighted when she had to remind me about her appointment.

SUCCESS AND MATURITY

I mentioned in the last chapter how our Orientation tends to shift as we pass through different stages in life. I mentioned Eric Erikson's eight life stages, each with its own tensions, with the tension between generativity and stagnation the one that most executives experience at the height of their careers. I mentioned as well how wisdom from our religious traditions shares this idea of transitions from one life stage to the next, and how Jungian psychology divides life into a first half – dedicated to conventional success – and a second half that's best committed to living according to the needs of our truest self. Each stage brings its own definitions of success. It's worth exploring, at any point in life, if how we think about success fits with our deepest callings.

I like Jung's approach because it is simple and backed by research. Data shows that happiness over our life tends to follow a shallow U, or a smile. We are relatively happy when we are young, carefree and discovering the world.

For all our adolescent angst, statistics show that our happiness only really dips when we reach our mid-20s and we begin to shoulder heavier responsibilities. Our happiness tends to continue to dip through our 30s and 40s. During these years, we feel most the weight of our careers, families, and demands to achieve and excel. One commentator calls these the 'shit gets real' years. He's not wrong. He's also not wrong to note that while the weight of our responsibilities may depress our happiness levels during these years, they are only one part of the journey. In the late 40s and early 50s – what Jung would call the transition years from the first half of life to the second half of life – we reach the lowest point of our happiness levels. And then things typically begin to shift for the better. By that time, we have often reached good levels of conventional success and perhaps a degree of financial security. The relationships that we invested in begin to settle and even flourish. We have more time to think about our legacy. Importantly, our ability to understand who we truly want to be once the responsibilities of conventional success are left behind is helped by all that we learn about ourselves in the first half of life. Jung called this journey to our truest self in the second half of life the journey of individuation, the true and honest work of understanding who we really are. My work is often to help leaders become more coherent to their sense of who they would like to be, once they shed the skin of the person they think they are expected to be. This is where transitions work is especially useful. Our leadership transitions are perfect opportunities for us to test how our personal definitions of success might shift given the new chapter ahead of us. One way we explore how our definitions of success might need a change as we pivot to a new leadership challenge is to ask ourselves three questions:

1. In what ways was I successful in my last leadership chapter? What contributed to my success?
2. What wisdom can I take from this last chapter, and how might that wisdom help me as I start my next one?
3. What wisdom might I still be missing?

In this exercise, success is when we live as close as possible to the person we are when we express our wisest self. In leadership, wisdom shows up in increasingly mature ways as responsibilities get more important and more complex. Note that I am not talking about knowledge, or even expertise. I am referring to the integration into our work of all that we have learned about who we are, what matters most to us, our weaknesses and our strengths.

THE SMALL ACTIVITIES THAT GIVE US THE GREATEST SENSE OF RENEWAL, JOY, HAPPINESS, OPTIMISM AND LOVE

With this last Roots question, we turn to a strange irony: we are likely to forget the small joys of our lives just when we need them the most. The quotations from Tedeschi and Calhoun at the beginning of this chapter all tell stories of trauma sufferers who remembered their deepest sources of joy because their trauma burnt away what was unimportant. Chaos distracts us toward self-preservation and away from joy – it's hard to appreciate the beauty of the jungle when a tiger is chewing on your leg. When we suffer from too much chaos in our lives, we concentrate so much on our survival that we forget to nurture our deepest sources of joy. We forget what is essential to our deepest sense of fulfilment. In a way, chaos distracts us from watering our Roots.

Our forgetfulness shows up in different ways. Important family events slip our minds. We set aside essential relationships. We ignore old hobbies. One leader tells the story of how she used to paint but doesn't have the time or energy or space for it these days. Another client talks about how the overwhelming pressure of his leadership keeps him away from spending even a little time in his beloved mountains. A third remembers how she once spent hours every week writing poetry, but doesn't any more because who has the time.

I had similar experiences. I remember once standing on the side of a perfectly groomed ski slope on a brilliant winter day in Zermatt on a family ski vacation, typing away an angry email message on my phone because some colleague was mounting a public attack on my work. I remember responding to one of my adversaries on my mobile phone during a Bruce Springsteen concert in Geneva. A colleague had warned me that they were about to launch another series of complaints against my team. I felt I had to get ahead of the attack, no matter that Springsteen was playing a fantastic version of "Thunder Road" in the background at the time. It seems like silly behaviour now, but whatever shame I felt because of it disappeared when I understood that it is exactly the behaviour we would expect from someone who feels under attack.

I'll briefly describe three approaches we use to guide our exploration of this aspect of our Root system. They all focus on identifying the activities that renew us.

First, remember the activities that gave you the most joy when you were ten years old. We already have a lot of wisdom when we are ten years old. We have enough of our childhood behind us to understand what we like and what we don't like, but we haven't yet been lost in the narrative rebellion and emerging myth-making of our adolescence. Here I borrow language from narrative researcher Dan McAdams. McAdams writes: "Our favourite stories usually contain those motifs and themes that we are most strongly attracted as children."[49] So, after reading these words, close your eyes and imagine the 'you' you were when you were ten years old. What did you do when you weren't at school or doing family chores? What captivated your imagination? What sorts of activities or hobbies kept you occupied for hours and hours? Was it sports? Art? Nature? I remember as a young, nerdy, freckle-faced kid loving sports, but also getting lost for hours wandering around the neighbourhood creek, looking for frogs and tadpoles and climbing trees. I remember taking pictures of the squirrels that used to come close enough to almost feed by hand, imagining that I was a wildlife photographer on some journey to the African savannah (not sure if they have squirrels there, but that didn't matter to my ten-year-old imagination). I would explore and explore and explore, and I remember how this need to explore the new and the wonderful had atrophied because of my work demands.

The idea isn't to pick up again the activities that kept you occupied when you were ten. The idea is to recognize and feed the deep parts of you that needed expression when you were young and might still need expression now. Taking pictures of squirrels wouldn't quite work for me now. But the need to explore, to examine and understand and appreciate, is still there. I ignore it at my peril.

Second, remember the activities that you've relied on to renew and refresh you in the past years but which you may have forgotten during your leadership transition.

This question requires a little less imagination to answer. I've already written about how I'd lacked the discipline or mental fortitude to keep the pressures of my leadership transition out of my ski holidays, concerts and family space. Even conversations at the family dinner table became fixated on my work. I remember one humbling family dinner when my young stepson Antoine wondered out loud if it might be good to talk about something other than my work when we gathered around the kitchen table for our evening meals. He wasn't angry and he wasn't blaming me. He was just concerned, as kids can be, that I was being possessed by something that was taking me away from the me he loved and needed. Remembering the activities that captured our imaginations before they were distracted by the demanding work of our transitions is the first step toward keeping a place in our lives for them.

If I were to make a list of five activities I wish I'd kept in my life during my painful leadership transition, I'd include:

- Going for more walks or hikes with Rox, and only using some of that walking time to process what was going on at work. We have a good practice of hiking in the fields and forests near our small village.
- Writing, imaginatively and creatively, and not just about leadership. Maybe a little active imagination writing to explore some unexplored parts of my life.
- Reading, for fun – fiction or history or anything that took my imagination away from work stress. I took a course on children's literature once, so maybe more of that.
- Running, skiing and climbing, all of which take my brain away from protective mode and put it into the present challenge of navigating the slope or manoeuvring myself up a rock wall.

- Helping Rox and Antoine or anyone else close to me with whatever challenges they were facing. The science is clear on the psychological benefits of helping others. It's just hard to remember to think of others when we're preoccupied with our own survival.

Third, think about what you would be doing with your time if you had no financial or social limitations. I like the playfulness of this exercise. It invites the elephant into the imaginative work. By letting our imagination know that for the purposes of this exploration we don't need to worry about real-life obligations, we let our riders take a break. When we dive into the exercise with executives, they usually find it hard to put aside their obligations. Once they do, though, the elephant often steps in with a flood of ideas. Recent responses have ranged from museum curator, travel writer, football coach and surf instructor in Portugal (bizarrely, twice in the space of a week from two very different leaders) to video game designer, master chef and round-the-world sailor. We don't pay too much attention to the activity. We do pay attention to why the activity is meaningful and renewing for the leader. Often these activities represent unexpressed spirits in the executive – a desire to care for something, grow something, make a creative difference – that deserve much more attention.

*Life comes from physical survival;
but the good life comes from
what we care about.*

**- ROLLO MAY,
*LOVE AND WILL***

SUMMARY

If our Orientation helps us understand the 'why' of our leadership, our Roots describe the 'how.' Our Root system includes our deepest values and most essential beliefs. In leadership, our Roots guide our behaviour, lead us through difficult choices, and show the people around us what we stand for. Our Orientation directs us toward a future that is better than the present, thanks to our leadership. Our Roots keep us stable and strong no matter how difficult the path of our Orientation might be.

When we explore our Roots, we face two challenges. First, our beliefs and values are difficult to define and prioritize. Their deeper meaning hides behind easy labels, and it is not always clear where each value sits on our value hierarchy. Second, our most important beliefs and deepest values are often unexplored. We don't know where they come from, if they are really ours, or if we've inherited them from somewhere or someone else.

We explore three territories to help our rider make sense of material that usually sits in our elephant. First, we explore the origin and meaning of our core beliefs and essential values. Second, we test each of them against the ways in which we define success in our leadership and in our life. Third, we explore how our beliefs and values are present in the small and sometimes forgotten activities that give us greatest access to our most positive emotions.

Before we turn to Relationships, the East point of the Leader's Compass, sketch down your answers to the following Roots questions.

1. List five beliefs and values that define your approach to leadership. Are any of them new? Do any of them feel like they might have outlived their usefulness?[50] List them as if they were the only way you could define your leadership to someone who looks up to you.

2. Describe how you would have defined success in your life and in your leadership ten years ago. Describe how you would define it now. Be specific about the type of evidence that would suggest that you are successful, according to your definitions. Now define success according to your Orientation. How is this definition different from the last one? If so, what does the difference suggest about how your beliefs or values might need to change?

3. List the small activities, hobbies, habits, routines or passions that gave you the most joy when you were ten years old. Recreate the list for when you were 30. Recreate it for who you are now. Is today's list longer or shorter than the list you created for ten-year-old you? Is there anything missing from today's list? Which of these small activities still get the attention they need, despite the busyness of your leadership?

CHAPTER 6

RELATIONSHIPS (EAST)

THE WISE NARRATIVE OF YOUR OUTER AND INNER CONNECTIONS

Another experience often reported by trauma survivors is a need to talk about the traumatic events, which sets into motion tests of interpersonal relationships – some pass, others fail. They may also find themselves becoming more comfortable with intimacy and having a greater sense of compassion for others who experience life difficulties.

- RICHARD G. TEDESCHI AND LAURENCE CALHOUN,
POSTTRAUMATIC GROWTH IN CLINICAL PRACTICE

If Orientation and Roots form the North-South axis of the Leader's Compass, Relationships and Resources form the East-West axis. It's useful to think about the North-South axis as our *meaning* axis because it covers the activities, values and beliefs that help us understand if we are leading a meaningful life. It's also useful to think of the East-West axis as our *engagement* axis since our Relationships and Resources shape the quality of our engagement with the world and ourselves.

Almost all the schools of psychology identify Relationships as key to our psychological stability. The American Psychological Association describes the importance of 'building your connections' and 'prioritizing genuinely connecting with people who care about you' as important to our psychological resilience. Studies of seniors show a clear link between social isolation and degraded mental and physical health. All five of the schools of psychology I covered in my research indicate that high-quality Relationships are critical to our psychological wellbeing and that nurturing them is an essential evolutionary drive. We live in social structures. Finding personal meaning and high-quality connection within these structures is a critical component of what it means to be human. When the social structures we rely on to feel safely engaged with the world around us break down, we are psychologically vulnerable.

We might think that we are immune to this vulnerability at work, where our Relationships might feel more transactional than deeply human, but we would be mistaken. For reasons we will explore later in this chapter, high-quality Relationships are especially important in the work setting, and especially important when we are leading people who depend on us for psychological security. Researchers of mobbing – the nonsexual harassment of an individual by a group of coworkers for the purpose of removing the targeted individual from the organiza-tion[51] – note how the most painful consequence of the experience is the sense of betrayal by once-trusted col-leagues. They note that "without collegial or coworker support, the mobbed worker is left in a very isolated situ-ation, experiencing further betrayal and shame."[52] When we can't count on the quality of our Relationships at work to protect us from pathological behaviour, our psycho-logical security suffers, sometimes catastrophically.

Post-trauma growth psychology gives a special empha-sis to the *quality* of Relationships, not just their number, as key to the process of growing through transition. Tak-ing a relevant example from Calhoun and Tedeschi:[53]

> A senior executive was diagnosed with a rare and serious form of cancer. His treatment required periodic leaves from work, so his condition became well-known to his coworkers. As the cycle of treatment, home for recovery and return to work continued, he found himself focusing on what he called "the deeper stuff." When colleagues at work greeted him with a routine "how are you doing," he found himself wanting to avoid inconsequential social pleasantries and, at least with colleagues who seemed really interested, he began to speak honestly about things. He began to tell them a bit more about his treat-ment, what it was like, talking more with them about some of "the deeper stuff." As one of those colleagues indicated, there was a reciprocal increase in meaningful responses from others, who then began to tell the exec-utive about their own "deeper stuff" – particularly about their concern and care for him in his battle with cancer.

By quality of Relationships, Calhoun and Tedeschi mean the openness and honesty with which people who have suffered through difficult transitions manage their connections with those they value most. Openness and honesty are important indicators of Relationship quality that I'll return to later in the chapter, and it's worth giving another example from their work to illustrate the point:

> A widow we interviewed some years ago said, "I feel much freer to express my emotions now, because I went through a time when I couldn't hold them back anyway. And now I like that I can let them flow with people I trust." There can be a greater sense of freedom to talk about one's thoughts and feelings, but also a greater sense of allowing oneself to let others see feelings and emotions. The encounter with suffering can lead people to be more honest, at least with trusted others, about how they feel and think, and to experience greater ease in expressing themselves emotionally to others.[54]

We will turn to three territories to explore our Relationships. You'll notice that none of the territories includes the typical stakeholder mapping that we often find in transitions manuals. While mapping the needs of our most important stakeholders is undoubtedly useful, my focus here is on the quality of the Relationships that are *most psychologically critical* to the transitioning leader rather than Relationships that are tactically helpful.

Our three territories are:

1. **The quality of your Relationships with the people who are your secure bases, and with the people for whom you are a secure base**
2. **The quality of your Relationship with your organization**
3. **The quality of your Relationship with yourself**

THE QUALITY OF YOUR RELATIONSHIP WITH THE PEOPLE WHO ARE YOUR SECURE BASES, AND WITH THE PEOPLE FOR WHOM YOU ARE A SECURE BASE

For this territory to make sense, I will need to explain what I mean by a 'secure base.' I'll start with a personal story. Years ago, not long after I moved from Canada to Switzerland, I fell in love with the mountains. The love first started when I read a book about the history of the north face of the Eiger, a famous mountain in the Swiss Bernese Oberland that was the stage for some of mountaineering's most touching and terrifying dramas from the early days of Alpine climbing. My preferred spot for learning how to climb was Chamonix, a bustling and beautiful small town in the French Alps nestled at the foot of Mont Blanc, western Europe's tallest mountain. I loved (and still love – I am typing these words in the kitchen of a friend's chalet on the outskirts of town) the vibe in Chamonix, although my enthusiasm for the idea of mountain climbing stumbled in the face of my lack of natural talent. Nevertheless, over many years I persisted with climbing and managed to spend endless days up in the mountains testing myself, scaring myself, vowing never to do this again (*Why am I way up here on this stupid mountain when I could be down in Chamonix having a beer?*) and, importantly, always going back up.

A huge contributor to my love of mountaineering was the mountain guide who was with me on almost every climb. His name is Olivier Greber. Olivier is originally from Alsace but came to the Chamonix valley in his youth. He loved it so much that he decided to make a career out of sharing the beauty of the mountains with others.

He put himself through all the necessary training and eventually qualified to be a guide in the Guides Office in Chamonix, a 200-year-old organization that first formed to take both tourists and serious climbers into the neighbouring peaks. Olivier and I connected through a strange set of circumstances that led to me becoming his client.

I'd heard stories from friends about their difficult experiences with mountain guides – that the guides they'd used were often impatient, unfriendly, even contemptuous of their clients – but my experience with Olivier was wonderful from the start. Something about him encouraged me to always return to the discomfort of our climbs. I put it down to his unwavering patience and good spirit, but I now know there was much more to his demeanour than just an easy-going friendliness. I know this because developmental psychologists have studied how we are wired to explore and engage with the world – how we take risks, when we do it in a healthy way and why we might do it in an unhealthy way. They discovered the importance of having what they now call 'secure bases' so that we feel comfortable enough to face the challenges of the unknown in a healthy way.[55]

The original researchers into what became known as attachment theory studied how young children react to strange and potentially threatening situations. They discovered that the quality of engagement with potential threat – something we need to be able to do in order to grow – depends in large part on the quality of our attachments to our primary caregivers, the people who we instinctively depended on to protect us and guide us in our earliest years. The more secure that attachment is, the more likely we are to develop healthy mechanisms for observing the world around us, judging risk as we engage with it, and engaging with it in a way that helps us grow.

BEING A SECURE BASE

I'll use my experience with Olivier to illustrate an example of what it means to be a secure base. Let's imagine that I am scrambling up on a rock face with Olivier. Let's imagine that I haven't climbed this particular route before. Let's also imagine that I find myself on a pitch that feels beyond my capabilities. I'm stuck. And the more I hesitate, the more my legs shake and the more I feel the terror of falling off my stance. As usual, Olivier has already gone ahead in the pitch and secured himself to the rock wall, and a rope connects the two of us. His job at this moment is to *belay* me – to keep the rope between us tight enough so that if I fell, I'd fall safely. Let's imagine that as I grapple with my predicament, toes perched against a thin ridge in the rock and fingers losing their frail purchase on a small edge in the rock face, I follow my usual instinct to turn toward my primary caregiver – in this case Olivier – for cues on what to do next.

According to attachment theory, Olivier can react in four ways. Only one of them helps me grow.

He could be paying attention to someone or something else and so not notice my struggles. In this case, I'm unable to pick up cues from him about what to do or how to do it. I'm left to my own devices and, in this case, very likely to fail.

He could be overly protective. He could suggest that I back away from the challenge – the equivalent of a worried parent dissuading their child from ever taking on the risk of exploring the world – in which case I learn to turn away from even the healthy risks that will enable me to test myself and grow. I learn to avoid the challenge and turn away from the possibility of growth.

He could vary his response, perhaps by being protective in one situation, absent in the next, dismissive in the third. Faced with this inconsistency, I become confused about the appropriate course of action. I don't learn anything because it's difficult to make sense of the contradictory signals I'm getting from him. Inconsistent reactions from my primary caregiver teach me that there are no good ways to take on the world.

Or Olivier could behave in a way that helps me take on the risk and grow because of it. In the words of developmental psychologists, he could act as my secure base.

According to the developmental psychologists who studied the reactions of young children who were put in strange situations and who instinctively turned to their primary caregiver for support and guidance, being a secure base – as a parent, a leader and a mountain guide – means displaying six behaviours. Three of the behaviours *secure* the people who are looking to us for cues on how to engage with the world. Three of the behaviours help them *grow*. Olivier's gift to me was to show me all six of these behaviours often enough that I was willing to continue to take on the discomfort of climbing for the joy of growth that it brought to me.

Three <u>securing</u> secure base behaviours are *calmness*, *presence* and *caring*.

1. **Calmness** means that no matter how stressed I am on our climbs or how worried I am by the real or imagined dangers that I think we are facing, Olivier remains calm and relaxed. His calmness sooths the part of me that imagines all sorts of terrible outcomes. If he isn't worried, a small part of me knows that I also don't have to be worried.

2. **Presence** means that Olivier always pays attention to how I am doing during our climbs. He is aware of my mental state, he understands my physical state,

he knows if I am having a bad day or a good day, and he can sense how close I am to my limits. I know that he is paying attention, and I also know that he will moderate his behaviour according to the state I happen to be in.

3. **Caring** means that I know that Olivier is invested in my growth. I know that he feels the essence of his work is to help his clients enjoy the beauty of the mountains in a way that only people who test themselves in them can. He knows that understanding the deep beauty of it all is the point of our experience together. And I know, explicitly, that Olivier wants to help me use the challenge of the mountains to test myself. He cares about the outcomes that I care about, and he cares about them just as deeply as I do.

Three <u>growing</u> secure base behaviours are *challenging*, *guiding* and *encouraging*.

4. **Challenging** means not removing the discomfort of testing ourselves. Olivier is not invested in my comfort. He is invested in my growth. We choose our climbs so that I will be tested, so that I will always feel the tension of being on the edge. He knows that important growth can happen if I am forced to adjust myself to the discomfort of a difficult challenge.

5. **Guiding** means showing possible approaches for taking on the challenge. For Olivier, guiding means not just taking us up the right route, but also suggesting where I might find my next handhold or a small correction in my skiing technique so that I can take on my challenges with slightly more expertise. For a parent,

guiding means showing your child how they might do things a little differently next time – say petting rather than painfully poking the new family dog – so that they increase their chances for a good outcome. For a leader, it means asking good exploratory questions and suggesting possible approaches for the people you lead based on the wisdom you've learned through your own hard experience. For Olivier, it means sharing his wisdom about what techniques work and don't work when we are in the mountains.

6. **Encouraging** is sharing a positive and optimistic spirit about what is possible, what might lay ahead with a little practice and persistence. Encouragement means instilling confidence. It also means showing the people that look to you for cues on how to approach their challenges that they are capable of more than they might think, and that no matter how intimidating or overwhelming their challenges might feel, they are up to the task. Olivier is endlessly encouraging when we are taking on a climb, full of so many helpful phrases that they are now a running joke between us.

LEADERSHIP TRANSITIONS AND SECURE BASES

Attachment theory suggests that we continue to rely on the quality of our Relationships with the people who are important to us into adulthood. This gives us two reasons for leaders in transition to pay attention to it. First, as we're taking on our transitional challenges, we will need our own secure bases intact so that we keep ourselves psychologically stable. Second, we need to pay attention to our own importance as a secure base to the people we lead, keeping in mind that we might become so preoccupied by our own challenges that we forget to demonstrate secure base behaviour to the people who need it most.

As you're preparing for and undertaking your leadership transition, reflect on the current quality of the secure base behaviour that you receive and that you give. It's useful to reflect on the state of your Relationship both as a giver and as a receiver of secure base behaviour. Two explorations might help:

First, reflect on the current state of your Relationships with the people in your life who've acted as your secure bases. Your secure bases might be your partners, friends, members of your family, mentors and coaches. Think of anyone who has consistently demonstrated calmness, presence and caring toward you, and who challenges you, guides you and encourages you. How many of these people exist in your life? What is the state of your Relationship with each of them? Does it need more attention? Can you lean on them to help you work your way through your leadership transition?

Remember, you don't need many secure bases and, as we will see later in this chapter, you can also act as your own secure base. Two or three secure bases are usually enough. The challenge is not in how many you have, but rather in nurturing your Relationships with your secure bases so that they remain available to you during your transitions.

Second, reflect on the people who rely on you as a secure base. If your leadership transition is in the form of a new role, this group will include all the people you now lead. If it is in the form of changing business circumstances, it will include all the people who will benefit from your calmness, presence, caring, and from the challenges, guidance and encouragement that you give them during the chaos of change. Who is in this group?

Who needs you most? Which of the six secure base behaviours do you consistently provide to them? Which could you provide more of or more consistently?

THE QUALITY OF YOUR RELATIONSHIP WITH YOUR ORGANIZATION

This territory might seem strange. Organizations aren't people. We don't really have Relationships with them. We work, we make a living. But, for better or for worse, our engagement with the organizations we work within aren't so simple. In an earlier chapter, I described how organizational life can give us comforting answers to some of life's most uncomfortable questions. The organizations we work within can give us a sense of meaning in our lives. They can give us a community of people with whom we share a significant part of our waking hours. They can give us a structure to guide our behaviour and regulate our activities. If we are a leader, they can give us a sense of being special and, therefore, perhaps at least a little immune to life's randomness. Our work can make us feel important and it can be agonizingly difficult, almost impossible, to put that sense of importance at risk.

For this reason, we often find that leaders are unwilling to view their Relationship with the organization that employs them as a Relationship of equals. Instead, they feel that they need to please the organization more than the organization needs to please them. Alex, whose story I described briefly in the chapter on wise narratives, is a great example of this unconscious reflex. Alex took on a new role with energy, enthusiasm and the dry sense of humour which had served him well. He soon found himself the target of a political attack from a member of his team who accused him of behaviour that Alex didn't recognize in himself and that, for deeply personal reasons, was exactly the kind of behaviour that he had fought against earlier in his career. His organization responded with an excess of caution, awarding the team member with a generous exit package and punishing Alex financially by withholding his bonus, all the while keeping him in the dark about the exact nature of the accusations against him.

During our conversations, Alex spoke about how much he enjoyed his work and how he didn't want to leave the organization. He also spoke about the pain that he suffered because he felt that he was being treated unfairly, even humiliated, at the hands of the organization. We talked about what would be different for him if he reframed his Relationship with the organization so that they were equals in the Relationship – that as much as the organization felt that it had the right to make demands of him, he also had just as much right to make demands of the organization. What demands would he make of the organization's leaders? What behaviours would he expect of them? How would he ensure that in his dance with the organization, neither partner was always taking the lead?

We might feel as if our rider manages our engagement with our organizations, but our elephants are active participants. To explore the extent to which our elephants are engaged with the company we work for, we explore two territories. We open the door to the first territory with the question: *To what extent are you sacrificing the person you want to be in order to please your organization?* We open the door to the second territory with the question: *What would you be doing if you weren't working in your current role in your current company?*

DEVELOPING AN ADULT-TO-ADULT RELATIONSHIP WITH YOUR ORGANIZATION

Like Alex, I had an unequal Relationship with the organization I belonged to when I undertook my leadership transition. I viewed my organization as something I needed to please, and I was willing to bend myself out of shape to please it. Part of the reflex might have been my lack of maturity or confidence. Part of it might have been because I had been at the organization for so long that it felt strange for me to think about not being there any longer. And an important part of it was undoubtedly that organizations are structured in hierarchies and hierarchies are excellent at encouraging parent-child Relationships.

The parent-child concept comes from transactional analysis, a study of the ego states that tend to be at play when human beings relate to one another.[56] Three common ego states are the parent, the child and the adult. The parent and child ego states come with all sorts of positive attributes – the loving parent, the learning child – but they also come with less helpful attributes – the domineering parent and the submissive, eager-to-please child. In organizational settings, for example, being in the less-helpful Relationship dynamic might mean that the employee (the child) is overly eager to please the demanding parent (the organization, often in the guise of its senior leaders). A healthy parent-child Relationship with the organization is better. But an adult-to-adult Relationship, where the leader and the company work as equals, is best.

Reaching an adult-to-adult Relationship with an organization that employs us can be difficult because our reflex is to please our sources of protection. For all sorts of reasons, deep in our elephant is the desire to find psychological stability in our Relationships with our parents (when we are very young) and then with our culture (once we realize that our parents are more vulnerable than we once thought). It's a natural reflex, but it's a reflex worth treating carefully. Organizations are not good curators of our core narratives or of our psychological wellbeing. Wisdom comes when we author our own narratives and insist on respectful treatment from everyone around us, including the organizations that we serve.

An interesting way to test the quality of your Relationship with your organization is to explore honest answers to an important question: *What inappropriate demands is my organization asking of me, and what appropriate demands am I not making of my organization?* There won't be perfect answers to the question, but there will be intuitions about the ways in which your organization might be bending you away from the person you could be, and likewise ways in which the organization should be bending itself into the right shape for you.

THE POWER OF AN ATTRACTIVE PLAN B

It's easier to avoid bending ourselves out of shape in our Relationship with our organization when we don't have to be there. Part of the anxiety that gripped my elephant during my difficult leadership work was because my options felt severely limited. I was married to a Swiss woman whose young son needed to stay close to his father. My French wasn't good enough to make working at a local organization viable, at least in the short term. And the kind of work I was doing catered to either the academic or the professional services worlds, none of which offered many local possibilities. When I was struggling with my leadership work, I had very few easy answers to the question: What will I do if I'm not doing *this*? This was fearful territory for the elephant. He imagined either moving away and breaking up the family or staying in Switzerland but not being able to find a suitable job and, therefore, having to sell the house and maybe live under a bridge somewhere (a vivid imagination and a scared elephant is a creative combination). My elephant wasn't sure if the skills I'd developed in the long years at my organization were transferrable, or if I'd somehow have to start over while I was edging up to 50.

It turns out that we can bring the best of ourselves to Plan A if we have a good Plan B. This doesn't mean that we have to exercise our Plan B, or that we don't apply ourselves fully to achieving success in our Plan A. It only means that if we find ourselves in an organization whose values are shifting away from ours, or whose leadership is asking us to become someone we don't want to be, we are less likely to make unwise compromises if we've gone to the trouble to explore our options outside of the organization.

We run into an understandable tension when we explore the concept of a good Plan B with leaders. There's an uneasiness associated with exploring possibilities outside of the current role – such explorations can feel disloyal, as if we're withholding some sense of commitment to the organization by casting our eyes outside of it. As we've already explored, organizations benefit from this sense of loyalty, even if it isn't returned. When we test the idea of having good options available, I encourage leaders to remember that their primary loyalty is to their wisest narrative – that is, to the work that aligns most closely with their Orientation (the difference they want to make) and that nurtures their Roots (their most important values, their wisest beliefs). Any role that carries them away from their deepest meaning is asking them to sacrifice too much.

Here we get to two challenges when we explore the possibility of a good Plan B. The first is the challenge of *marginal compromises*, and the second is the challenge of *ego and status over purpose*. Both of these challenges can seduce us into staying with a toxic Plan A.

By marginal compromises, I mean the small compromises that organization's might ask of us that don't seem too important at the time but which compound, until we no longer recognize who we are – or, worse, we recognize who we are but find what we see so unbearable that we hide behind dishonest rationalizations. I've seen this reflex hard at work with leaders who aren't far from retirement and so protect what they hope will be comfortable final years at work. It's easier to rationalize away our compromises when we can pretend we're doing it for a good cause. The reflex shows up in the way we pretend to agree with decisions that we know are wrong, or when we treat people in ways that compromise our values because that's what our leadership has asked us to do. It also shows up in how we agree to diminish ourselves, one small step at a time, in order to please people who don't deserve pleasing.

The best way to face the challenge of marginal compromises is to pay attention to them. Our elephants are helpful: they know when we are facing the possibility of edging up against compromises that will cost us too much. They may not trumpet loudly when these compromises come up, but they will speak to us, often quietly, so that we know that they are there. Once we know that we might be stepping deeper into a minefield of compromises, it's easier to find wise ways to step our way out.

The challenge of ego and status is related to the challenge of marginal compromises. Ego and status are part of what we protect, sometimes unconsciously, as we think about what makes for a good Plan A and an equally good Plan B. We work hard to achieve status through our work, and it can be difficult to risk losing that status by risking our role to stay as aligned as possible to our Orientation and our Roots. If we find our need for status is met where we currently work, we can find ways to justify staying there, no matter how badly staying might take us away from our wisest selves. Since status gives us a sense (sometimes false) of protection against all sorts of psychological vulnerabilities, it's useful to make the dance of status versus Orientation a conscious one – that is, make sure that your rider and your elephant are taking on the conversation together.[57]

Four questions help us explore the current Relationship. They are:

- **How is your current work taking you away from your Orientation and starving your Roots?** Here we explore how the wise narrative of the leader's Orientation and Roots is satisfied by the current work, and how it is not satisfied. The point is to identify any compromises that might be driven by the seduction of status.

- **What about your current work makes this cost to your Orientation and Roots justifiable?** Here we go through the balancing act of understanding exactly what benefits come from the costs your Orientation and Roots are paying so that our ego feels satisfied.

- **What must you demand of your organization to minimize this cost?** This third exploration helps us understand how we can minimize the compromises we make in our Plan A, our current work, so that it isn't unnecessarily costly to us.

- **What about a new role – a Plan B – would make it worth the trouble of changing your job?** Here we think through the circumstances that would make stepping toward an attractive Plan B worth the challenge of changing organizations. We think carefully about the realistic benefits and risks associated with stepping toward Plan B.

It's worth noting again that the point of this work isn't to prepare for a career change. It is to make sure that you understand what good alternatives are available to you if the costs of staying where you are become unbearable. In keeping with all our Leader's Compass work, exploring answers to these questions helps us form the wise narrative of our career choices.

THE QUALITY OF YOUR RELATIONSHIP WITH YOURSELF

This final Relationship question might matter more than the first two. We can usually negotiate good Relationships with our secure bases and with our organization, and if we are wise, we can do this from a safe distance. It's more difficult to take a safe and detached distance from ourselves. Our elephants are often far too chaotic for us to hold them at a distance, and our rider's too protective of their privileged positions to make themselves transparent.

For efficiency's sake, I'll focus on the aspects of personal leadership that show up most often in our leadership transitions work. I'll start by introducing a theme that is so common that it hints at some deep dimension of what it means to be human. I'll also explore why it matters that we have a good Relationship with ourselves, what that might look like, and what we can do to become our own secure bases (to borrow from our attachment theory material earlier in the chapter).

THE VOICE THAT TELLS ME THAT I AM NOT ENOUGH

When we are comfortable enough to probe deeply into what's stirring below the surface of the leaders we support, one theme almost always shows up. The theme points to the quality of the Relationship the leader has with themselves.

The theme is the voice within us that tell us: *I am not enough.* Leaders refer to it as a vaguely disturbing sense of inadequacy, sometimes sitting in the background of their awareness and sometimes standing loudly at the forefront of their minds. The more we feel under threat – say, under the threat of taking on a new leadership role – the louder the voice gets.

The voice has multiple layers. The first layer is the most obvious. At its simplest, the voice is warning us that we are not *good* enough, *smart* enough, *handsome* enough, *agile* enough, *charming* enough – all of the things that we somehow imagine we should be, or that we need to be – to survive in our strange and confusing world. The voice is usually a voice that emerged in us to protect us when we were very young and when we began to realize that we needed to manage the hostility of the world around us. Canadian psychologist Gabor Maté refers to it as our 'stupid friend' voice: it means well, but it lacks wisdom to guide us with any real skill. Maté claims that the voice is our frightened four-year-old-voice, with all the wisdom and subtlety we had when we were four years old. It's important to remember that the voice is essentially protective. It sees the world around us as threatening, and it wants to protect us from the threat by encouraging us to be more than we are.

We find the voice's deeper meaning when we explore what wisdom it might be trying to share with us. With exploration, we understand that the voice is confusing because it is both *absolutely true* and *completely false.* It is true that none of us is enough to avoid the existential anxieties of life. No matter how charming, clever, agile or strong we are, we can't escape the randomness of life or the fact that it will end one day. Coming to terms with this fact is usually part of the passage into the second half of life. But before then, the strident voice inside of us that screams to us that we are not enough is a voice that wishes it weren't true, that if only we were *more* we would be free of life's inevitable turmoil. Unfortunately, this voice tends to confuse our inability to avoid the una-voidables of life with our ability to face our challenges, sometimes overcome them, sometimes fail, but always with the possibility of learning. If you ask this voice what it means by 'enough' and it struggles to give you a clear answer, there's a good chance it is confusing your exis-tential vulnerability with your ability to grow.

We can calm this young, anxious voice inside of us with a healthy dose of curiosity. We can ask it:

- **What are you trying to protect me from?** What threats am I facing, really? If I am a leader going through an important transition, what real threats do I face as I step into the new role?

- **Whose voice are you?** Are you the voice of the four-year-old me trying to protect me from imagined monsters, or are you the voice of the wisest me who is curious about what I might learn from the challenges that lie ahead?

- **What could I do to be 'enough'?** Are there any circumstances under which you would stop telling me that I am not enough? What are they? Who would I have to be to be enough to satisfy you?

- **How would the content and tone of your message to me change if you were the voice of the wisest part of me?** Would you recognize all that I've managed to overcome and achieve in my life? Would you acknowledge that not everything you see as a threat really is? Would you be a calmer and more reassuring voice?

DEVELOPING OUR WISEST INNER VOICE

This last question points to the importance of developing a wise Relationship with ourselves. Each of the five schools of psychology I explored in the research has its own version of this Relationship. Evolutionary psychology says that we get along better with ourselves when we understand the innate drives for survival, competition and reproduction that sit deep within our elephants. We take our behaviour a little less personally when we understand that anger, for example, can be helpfully framed as a natural and very human response to perceived threat. Existential psychology says that a good Relationship with ourselves rests on our ability to face head-on, with mindfulness of being, the four existential anxieties that are part of being human. Analytical psychology tells us that we understand ourselves best when we integrate into our consciousness all that we've repressed. Narrative psychology tells us that we need to understand the tone, imagery and content of our inner narratives to understand ourselves. Post-trauma growth clinical practice knows that we grow when we take on the hard work of creating the wise narrative of who we are and who we want to be.

An additional source from psychology is worth noting here. It comes from clinical practitioners who have observed what makes for a good Relationship between a therapist and the person seeking therapy. If one way of framing our best Relationship with ourselves is becoming our own skilled therapist, we have some things to learn from the therapist-client Relationship.

An essential source in this field is the American psychologist Carl Rogers, who believed in the power of a client-focused approach to therapy. Rogers lists some of what he has learned from his thousands of hours helping people through their mental distress. He found that he is most helpful to others when he remembers the following lessons. As you read them, think about how your Relationship with yourself might change if your inner voice also remembered and behaved according to these lessons.[58]

In my Relationships with persons, I have found that it does not help, in the long run, to act as though I am something I am not.

I find I am more effective when I can listen acceptantly to myself, and can be myself.

I have found it enriching to open channels whereby others can communicate their feelings, their private perceptual worlds, to me.

The more I am open to the realities in me and in the other person, the less I find myself wishing to rush in and 'fix things.'

Experience is, for me, the highest authority. The touchstone of validity is my own experience.

What is most personal is most general.

Life, at its best, is a flowing, changing process in which nothing is fixed.

Imagine if we managed our Relationships with ourselves based on Rogers' observations. Imagine if we were always honest with who we are and what we're feeling, if we listened to ourselves with curiosity and acceptance rather than judgment, if we tried to understand ourselves before rushing to 'fix' what we think might be wrong.

Imagine if we were sensitive to our deeper emotions when we explored our understanding of ourselves, and if we searched our experience for wisdom rather than just accept all that we've been told and taught.

Imagine if we understood that the experiences that we believe are most unique to us, especially the most joyous and most difficult experiences, are in fact common to all of us. And imagine if we understood that life is especially rich when we are in the flow of fascinating change and frightening transition. Imagine what our Relationship with ourselves would look and feel like if we recognized the wisdom of Rogers' observations.

In post-trauma growth practice, researchers write about the importance of being an "expert companion" to the person seeking trauma therapy. Rogers' list is an excellent guide for those of us who want to become more expert companions to ourselves.

BEING OUR OWN SECURE BASE

Rogers' list has a lot in common with the secure base behaviours that I described at the beginning of the chapter, so let's end with a reminder of those behaviours. Let's also imagine that we turn the secure-base behaviours toward ourselves, so that we act as our own secure base. I'll end this chapter on Relationships with six sets of questions. Each question is associated with one of the secure base behaviours.

Calmness. What would it be like for you to treat yourself with calmness, acceptance and unconditional positive self-regard?

Presence. What would happen if you spent a little more time being present with yourself, paying attention to how your rider and elephant are behaving, to your unconscious reactions to the events in your life, and especially to the circumstances in your life that feel new or threatening?

Caring. How would your Relationship with yourself change if you approached yourself with the care of a loving parent, a close friend or even a skilled therapist?

Challenging. What would be different in your life if you saw the challenges that you take on, including the challenge of your leadership transition, as voluntary challenges that you take on because they can help you grow?

Guiding. How could your wisest self, the self that has gained so much knowledge from your countless experiences, guide you through your current challenges? What would it tell you to help you?

Encouraging. What would your wisest self tell you in order to shift any negative protective emotions in you – emotions like fear, anger, anxiety and pessimism – to the more growthful emotions of hope, happiness, joy and optimism?

SUMMARY

We are a social species. We rely on our Relationships for meaning, comfort and security. Strong Relationships nurture our resilience and help us know ourselves better.

We explore the presence and quality of three categories of Relationship when we embark on leadership transitions.

We explore the quality of our Relationships with the people who act as our secure bases. Our secure bases fulfil a deeply human need for secure attachment when we are exploring the outside world. Their calmness, presence and caring stabilize us when the world around us is caught in chaos. Their guidance, encouragement and the way they challenge us helps us step into our exploration of chaos with confidence.

We explore the quality of our Relationship with our organization to ensure that it is a Relationship in which both partners benefit and neither partner compromises what is essential to them. Transactional analysis gives us a useful way to frame the quality of a healthy Relationship to our organization by telling us that it should be an adult-to-adult Relationship rather than a Relationship between a demanding parent and an eager-to-please child. Adult-to-adult Relationships are negotiated between equals. They are best negotiated when both partners are in the Relationship because they want to be.

We also explore the quality of Relationship the transitioning leader has with himself or herself. Here we take guidance from the clinical world, which encourages Relationships of support, of unconditional positive regard, as if we are someone we are responsible for nurturing and growing. Our self-Relationship requires attention to the quality of our inner voice, making sure that it is a wise voice rather than the voice of the overly protective inner child.

I turn to our final compass point in Chapter 7. Before we step into that territory, take some time to sketch out some preliminary answers to the following Relationship questions. As always, write down what first comes to mind without worrying about being coherent or too logical. Your rider and your elephant might be competing for a say in what you write. Let their voices come out in an unfiltered form.

1. Identify three or four people from among your friends, family, colleagues, mentors and coaches who might act as your secure bases. Which of the six secure base behaviours do they display that you find most helpful? How often to you connect with them? Are each of these Relationships active, or do some of them need nurturing? List each of the people, the behaviours you appreciate most from them, the current state of your Relationship with them, and what you might do to strengthen the Relationship as you embark on your transition.

2. Who depends upon you as their secure base? How many of these are new Relationships that come to you because of your leadership transition? What can you do to nurture your Relationship with them? List the people, the state of your Relationship with each of them, and the actions you can take to strengthen your connection with them.

3. Would you describe your Relationship with your organization as an adult-to-adult Relationship or a parent-child Relationship? Are you compromising too much of what feels essential to you to stay in the Relationship? If so, what actions can you take to shift the Relationship so that it feels more like a Relationship between equals?

4. What would you be doing professionally if you weren't in your current role? What attractive alternatives are available to you?

5. How would you describe your Relationship with yourself? Does your inner voice appreciate and encourage you, as if you are someone you are responsible for supporting and growing? Is it critical in a way that diminishes you rather than strengthens you? What would your inner voice be telling you if it were a wiser voice?

CHAPTER 7

RESOURCES (WEST)

THE WISE NARRATIVE OF YOUR TALENTS, CHARACTER STRENGTHS AND SOURCES OF GRATITUDE

The good life consists of deriving happiness by using your signature strengths every day in your main realms of living. The meaningful life adds one more component: using these same strengths to forward knowledge, power or goodness.

- MARTIN SELIGMAN,
AUTHENTIC HAPPINESS

The most hopeful message coming out of post-trauma growth research is the message of strength. We grow through our difficult transitions in part because they can show us how strong we are. Laurence Calhoun and Richard Tedeschi describe this optimistic message in the following way:

> The occurrence of such bad things can also, paradoxically, lead some people to experience a positive change in how they see themselves. A common way this positive change is described is in phrases like "I am much stronger than I ever imagined. If I am living through this, I can live through just about anything" and "I had to live with major suffering and little things don't get to me any more."
>
> This paradox of growth can be summarized with the phrase *more vulnerable, yet stronger.* Loss and suffering teach people, particularly those of us in the Western tradition of individualism, of belief in personal control, and of self-reliance, that bad things can happen to us, sometimes with no warning and in ways that permit us no control over the outcomes. Life crises remind us that difficult challenges are an inevitable part of life. But in the confrontation with major crises, some persons also come to the realization that they have the capabilities to cope and survive, and perhaps even prevail, that they did not realize they had. As Albert Camus once said, "In the midst of winter, I finally learned that there was in me an invincible summer."[59]

In this final point of the Leader's Compass, our Resources, we'll explore the territory of strengths – or, in Camus's words, the territory of our invincible summer. We'll do that by exploring another three territories:

1. **The skills or talents that enable you to make a difference**
2. **Your signature strengths**
3. **Your sources of gratitude**

You'll notice that the territories have a positive spirit to them. That positive spirit connects post-trauma growth with positive psychology. Positive psychology grew out of a belief that clinical work focused too much on treating what felt wrong and not enough on all that was right. The work of positive psychology sends the same message about taking wisdom out of our most difficult challenges that is so critical to post-trauma growth. In the case of positive psychology, the wise narrative of us always includes the narrative of the things that give us agency.

There is a danger of being seduced by new ageism in this territory of positive emotion. It's tempting to believe that if we remember the good things about ourselves, our lives will be better. Toxic positivity is real and harmful, and I'll do my best to avoid it here. But I will draw from the excellent work of positive psychology and especially of Dr Martin Seligman[60] to set the stage for the chapter. I'll do that by sharing what Seligman and his researchers discovered about the emotions associated with personal growth. I'll start with what they call the Happiness Formula.[61]

According to positive psychology, our happiness (H) is a function of our biologically set range (S), our circumstances (C), and factors that are under our voluntary control (V). In other words:

$$H = S + C + V$$

V is the focus of both post-trauma clinical work and positive psychology. It is also the focus of our Resources work. But before we get to V, I'll briefly cover what we mean by the other components of the formula.

Seligman calls H our "enduring levels of happiness." Here he differentiates between our moments of fleeting pleasure and our baseline (and less changeable) level of happiness. Think of H as our resting level of happiness, the way you'd think about our resting heart rate – it is the way we are without really trying. We can also think of H as a proxy for what positive psychology calls positive emotion: optimism, hope, love, joy. At the other end of our emotional scale are negative emotions: pessimism, anger, bitterness, hate. The point of positive psychology is to explore how we can operate as often as possible with a sense of positive emotion. This goal is compelling for trauma researchers because trauma typically elicits negative emotion. Trauma research is interested in positive psychology because it also claims that growth is more likely to be found when we experience positive (generative) emotion than when we experience negative (protective) emotion.

S is the biologically set range we have between our access to positive emotion and negative emotion. We can't do much about this range. Each of us has our genetically programmed range that we return to no matter which happy or sad events might momentarily raise us or bring us down. Win the lottery and we're likely to return to within our S range of biologically set happiness within a few short months. Get fired and we'll do the same. S accounts for about half of our level of enduring happiness.

Our biology is important, and it probably defines the limits of our enduring happiness, but it isn't our destiny. There are two other contributors to our levels of positive emotion that influence whether we tend to play at the upper or lower end of our happiness range. These are our circumstances (C) and how we use the time over which we have voluntary control (V).

Our circumstances (C) – seem to have relatively small influence on where we play within our set happiness range: between 8–15%, according to Seligman. Also according to Seligman, the changes in our circumstances that are likely to improve our enduring levels of happiness tend to be impractical, impossible or expensive:

If you want to lastingly raise your level of happiness by changing the external circumstances of your life, you should do the following:

1. Live in a wealthy democracy, not an impoverished dictatorship (a strong effect)
2. Get married (a robust effect, but perhaps not causal)
3. Avoid negative events and negative emotion (only a moderate effect)
4. Acquire a rich social network (a robust effect, although perhaps not causal)
5. Become religious (a moderate effect)

As far as happiness and life satisfaction are concerned, however, you needn't bother to do the following:

6. Make more money (money has little or no effect once you are comfortable enough to buy this book, and more materialistic people are less happy)
7. Stay healthy (subjective health, not objective health matters)
8. Get as much education as possible (no effect)
9. Change your race or move to a sunnier climate (no effect)[62]

So, we humans (and we leaders) all work within a biologically set range of positive emotion. The circumstances of our lives have little influence on where we play within that range. What is important are the voluntary variables (V). Seligman explains how the voluntary variables include how we interpret our past, our present and our future. He describes the importance of gratitude and forgiveness as sources of positive emotion for all three. Critically, he explains how the use of our strengths – he calls them signature strengths – is essential to where we play in our set happiness range. In his words, drawing from the quotation I used to introduce this chapter:

> The good life consists in deriving happiness by using your signature strengths every day in the main realm of living. The meaningful life adds one more component: using these same strengths to forward knowledge, power or goodness.[63]

Our three Resource territories address three areas in which positive psychology and clinical work in post-trauma growth intersect. A good and meaningful life

– or, for the purposes of our work, good and meaningful leadership – comes when, in the course of our leadership, we use our talents and our strengths for a meaningful and good purpose. What post-trauma growth calls our wise narrative, positive psychology calls the application of our Resources – our talents and strengths – in the service of a meaningful cause. As we undertake our leadership transitions, we have an opportunity to remember and reconsider how we are using our strengths for a meaningful outcome.

THE SKILLS OR TALENTS THAT ENABLE US TO MAKE A DIFFERENCE

Author and executive coach Marshall Goldsmith famously wrote that "what got you here won't get you there," referring to the danger of relying only on existing habits to carry leaders to greater success. He might be partly right, but it's also true that you won't get far in any transition if you forget all the talents or skills that have served you well so far.

In the chapter on Orientation, we worked on developing a high-resolution sense of the difference you want to make through your leadership. Here we identify the things in you that will help you make that difference. These are typically talents that you've nurtured over your career, the skills that have enabled you to get the right things done, the things about you that encourage the people you lead to pay attention to you. When we think about our talents or skills, it's useful to think at three different levels: our *technical skills*, our *baseline talents*, and what I'll call our *Orientation talents*.

The first set of skills are the skills we might develop through our education and work experience. In my case, I developed a good understanding of the basics of business through an economics degree and an MBA. I likewise developed some expertise in leadership and leadership development through being part of the leadership team of a small organization that was active in the field. My doctoral work gave me much deeper insight into how our brains function under chaos. My practice gives me important information about how these insights can help leaders use the chaos of their work to grow. We can think of all of these skills as technical skills, since they can be learned through education and applied to a specific field. Almost all leaders have a good portfolio of technical skills because almost all of them have grown into their leadership roles on the back of their technical or functional experience.

A little deeper than our technical skills sit our baseline talents. Think of your baseline talents as the talents you have and have developed that have less to do with technical expertise and more to do with your ability to operate successfully in your world and in your work. Senior leaders tend to share a set of baseline talents that help them be effective: good brains, strong analytical thinking, decent problem-solving, an ability to connect with people, develop a vision, and mobilize Resources. These are all important, and they are all good reminders that when we walk into the unknown territory of transition, we aren't without Resources. We have plenty of reasons to be confident.

Deeper still are our Orientation talents. These are the talents we were born with or have developed that apply specifically to our ability to operate effectively in the territory of our Orientation. Here it's useful to think of the impact your Orientation is asking you to make, and then think of the abilities you have that enable you to make that impact. In my case, my Orientation asks me to help leaders use the most difficult challenges of their work as a laboratory for profound personal exploration and growth. Some personal attributes help me be effective in the territory. For example:

- I care. Caring gives me the energy to explore the territory properly, no matter how confusing or challenging it might become.
- I want to be useful to leaders who might be badly disoriented by their work.
- I am curious, but not judgmental.
- I've developed a good understanding of how different schools of psychology think about how our minds operate under chaos. I integrate all of them in my practice.
- I'm also good at integrating the rider with the elephant, at helping them understand each other, at recognizing and honouring both.

YOUR SIGNATURE STRENGTHS

Seligman addresses a different kind of strength in his work on the voluntary contributors to positive emotion. He calls them signature strengths, by which he means our most prominent character strengths. He differentiates them from our talents in part because of their moral character, and in part because of what he sees as our ability to develop them no matter what our innate or genetic starting points. Unlike talents, our character strengths can be developed from almost nothing. And it is in the intentional development of these character strengths that we move ourselves higher within our range of positive emotion. As Seligman notes:

> To be a virtuous person is to display, by acts of will, all or at least most of the six ubiquitous virtues: wisdom, courage, humanity, justice, temperance and transcendence. There are several distinct routes to each of these six. For example, one can display the virtue of justice by acts of good citizenship, fairness, loyalty and teamwork, or humane leadership. I call these routes strengths, and unlike the abstract virtues, each of these strengths is measurable and acquirable.[64]

According to Seligman, two characteristics help us understand our signature strengths:

> First, a strength is a trait, a psychological characteristic that can be seen across different situations and over time. A one-time display of kindness in one setting only does not display the underlying virtue of humanity.
> Second, a strength is valued in its own right. Strengths often produce good consequences. Leadership well exercised, for example, usually produces prestige, promotions and raises. Although strengths and virtues do produce such desirable outcomes, we value a strength for its own sake, even in the absence of obvious beneficial outcomes. Remember that the gratifications are undertaken for their own sake, not because they may produce a squirt of felt positive emotion in addition. Indeed, Aristotle argued that actions undertaken for external reasons are not virtuous, precisely because they are coaxed or coerced.[65]

Seligman and his fellow researchers have identified 27 strengths sitting under six virtues.[66] Translating the research into the field of leadership and leadership development, Seligman would argue that you are more likely to enjoy your leadership work if you express these strengths. In the same way, you are more likely to benefit from your leadership transitions if you use them to calibrate which strengths you have used in the past, and which you might have the opportunity to exercise more in the course of your emerging leadership work. The challenge for leaders, especially leaders in transition, is to pay attention to how their work gives them a stage on which to exercise these strengths.

THE BEFORE, THE DURING AND THE AFTER OF SIGNATURE STRENGTHS

Seligman and Peterson identify the following strengths, each under a specific virtue or virtues:

- **Strengths of Wisdom and Knowledge:** *Creativity, Curiosity, Open-Mindedness, Love of Learning and Perspective (or Wisdom).*
- **Strengths of Courage:** *Bravery, Persistence, Integrity and Vitality.*
- **Strengths of Humanity:** *Love, Kindness and Social Intelligence.*
- **Strengths of Justice:** *Citizenship (social responsibility, loyalty, teamwork), Fairness and Leadership.*
- **Strengths of Temperance:** *Forgiveness and Mercy, Humility and Modesty, Prudence and Self-Regulation.*
- **Strengths of Transcendence:** *Appreciation of Beauty and Excellence, Gratitude, Hope, Humour and Spirituality.*

Our transitions give us an opportunity to pay special attention to how our strengths play out during our step into new territory. In my case, and in the case of many clients, the dance of signature strengths can be surprising, especially if our work tests our core narratives. I'd describe my most important signature strengths before my transition as perspective, kindness, citizenship and prudence. The stress of my transition brought a new set of strengths to bear: bravery, persistence and integrity to take on what became a long struggle against a few of the people that I believed were corrupting the organization; creativity, curiosity and open-mindedness when I turned toward a new career focus; and love, kindness, gratitude and hope as I took on the challenge of my emerging Orientation. Some of the new strengths that I started to exercise during the transition faded – after I passed through the battle with my old colleagues, the need for bravery became less urgent – but I know that they are there if I need them.

The theme of using transitions to test old character strengths and build new ones is common in our transitions work. Alex, who took on his own battle with an organization that he felt was treating him poorly, went through a similar strengthening experience. He needed enormous courage to demand better treatment from his organization. He needed persistence to see the process through, to not give into the easy temptation of stepping away from a role that he otherwise loved or of accepting the treatment he was receiving just for the sake of getting along. Having lived through the experience, Alex shares my feeling that we have a broader set of strengths from which to draw when we have been tested by our transitions. The stress of his transition called him to develop a new set of strengths, until he emerged stronger across a wider set of Seligman's characteristics. This might be yet another overlap between post-trauma growth and positive psychology: we grow through trauma or transition when it enables us to develop new signature strengths.

YOUR SOURCES OF GRATITUDE

A final contribution from Seligman's work comes in the form of gratitude. Gratitude is included as a strength within the virtue of Transcendence (see list above), along with Hope, Humour, Spirituality, and Appreciation of Beauty and Excellence. Seligman writes about gratitude as a practice that plays a particularly powerful role in access to positive emotion. In fact, he lists two practices – the practice of *gratitude* and the practice of *forgiveness* – as sources of positive emotion when we go about re-interpreting or rewriting the experiences of our past. Here Seligman observes what post-trauma growth researchers and narrative psychologists have also noted: that we have tremendous power to hold our countless experiences at a distance and interpret them in infinite ways, and that wisdom comes when we interpret them not just for the pain they might have brought us, but also from how they might have helped us grow. How much wisdom we take from an experience is, in part, a function of how we interpret the story. David Denborough makes this power of detachment and (re)interpretation part of his therapeutic work.[67] Like Dan McAdams' work and the work of other founders of narrative therapy, Denborough's practice focuses on the possibility of multiple interpretations of experience, including positive interpretations of even the most difficult challenges. McAdams writes that we can't know ourselves unless we know our stories. This is true, in a narrative therapy sense, but the comment emphasizes the need to really *know* our stories: to explore them, play with them, hold them in our hands, and find multiple possibilities in each of them. It isn't a simple task. The elephant can get in the way, depending on what it is protecting. So too can the rider, also depending on what sense of control and mastery it is trying to preserve. But it is an important task. Seligman would claim that it is a task best taken on through a lens of gratitude.

I'll explain by sharing an inflection point in my own leadership transition. I'll do this by integrating some wisdom from Seligman and McAdams, both of whom share a perspective on how we translate our experiences into stories in order to make meaning out of them.

As I was being dragged deeper and deeper into the frustration of my leadership battle, I noticed that I had started to interpret older stories of my life through a darker lens. For example, I had travelled around the world with my family in the first 18 years of my life, thanks to my father's work as a diplomat for the Canadian government. His postings took my mother, my older brother, my older sister and me to many different countries on many different adventures – to France, Jamaica, West Germany and Israel, where he served as the Canadian Ambassador and where I finished high school. For most of my life, I'd thought of all of this travelling in a mostly positive sense. I'd thought that we were lucky to have had the opportunity to live all around the world, immerse ourselves in different cultures, and have our close family unit as an important ordering mechanism that kept secure as we moved from place to place. Whatever complaints I might have had about myself or about my circumstances, none of them had to do with these early years of my life. I felt grateful for the many experiences we shared.

That is, until I started to think differently about how I grew up. During my leadership battles, I began to think of our many moves as a source of restlessness and rootlessness. I imagined that part of the reason I didn't really understand how to make sense of my leadership battle was because I'd spent too much of my childhood trying to fit in rather than forming a stronger personal identity. I began to think that being the youngest child of three meant that I had grown up under the curse of always being smaller, weaker, more invisible. I began to think of our faith not as a source of wisdom but rather as an oppressive ideology. As my leadership transition brought me into darker territory, my interpretation of my life, especially my early life, became darker.

Before we get to the power of gratitude to brighten our interpretative lenses, I'll share some wisdom from Dan McAdams' work about how we create our personal narratives – our personal myths, as McAdams likes to call them. According to McAdams, we are all constantly creating the myth of our lives. Our myths change as we gain experience and become wiser, and they tend to change dramatically as we live through life's more dramatic inflection points. Adolescence, for example, or living through a nuclear event (McAdams' term) that significantly shapes our sense of who we are. Through all of our lives, however, our personal myth-making is guided by two opposing needs: the need to be personally powerful and the need to connect with other people. Our myths tend to gravitate to one of these needs, or to both, or to neither.

McAdams used the term 'imago' (pronounced im-EH-go) to explain how our myths conjure up inner characters that capture the spirits that express themselves in our story-making. Imagoes are the characters in our personal myths that represent different aspects of ourselves.

Some of our imagoes represent the parts of us that cherish the personal power we need to protect ourselves and the people we love. McAdams mentions The Warrior, The Traveller, The Sage and The Maker as agentic imagoes that show up in classic mythology (as Ares, Hermes, Zeus and Hephaestus, respectively). He likewise identifies The Lover (Aphrodite), The Caregiver (Demeter), The Friend (Hera) and the Ritualist (Hestia) as communal/connective imagoes. Some of our inner characters combine both personal power and communal power: McAdams mentions the Healer, Humanist, Teacher and Counsellor as bringing together our personal and communal power. And finally, he mentions the characters inside of us that are neither agentic nor communal: The Survivor, The Escapist, and one that I'll add to his list, The Victim. This last category of inner character is one that we all have inside of us, but it is the one that serves our growth the least because it harnesses neither our agentic nor our communal energy. Gratitude, it turns out, encourages our agentic and communal myth-making and discourages victimhood. Gratitude keeps us in a spirit of growing, whether we shine it on our past, our present, or our sense of what the future may hold for us.[68]

The beauty of McAdams' imago work is that he encourages us to imagine our own agentic and communal characters. He asks us to picture them, name them, and play with how and when they show up on our inner stage. He asks us to imagine how our inner stage might look if we rebalanced our cast of inner characters, especially when it has been thrown out of an old equilibrium because of some external event.

In my case, that external event was my leadership transition. If I walked into the transition with a solid (and overused) communal character – let's call it my Diplomat, the strength in me that got along with people, that tried to keep a wise perspective, and sometimes tried too hard to please – I learned quickly that I needed some agentic strength to fight my fight. Unfortunately, my inner Warrior was underdeveloped and, therefore, neither nuanced nor wise. It sometimes showed up with a little too much anger, sometimes with too much brutal honesty, sometimes just confused about how to act. As my Warrior and old Diplomat tried to sort themselves out, both retreated from the inner stage. Victimhood stepped in. It wasn't until I read Seligman's wisdom about gratitude that I was able to create a new equilibrium of equally strong characters on my inner stage. I turned my gaze of gratitude to my past and developed a wiser narrative about my adventurous childhood that was neither overly romantic nor cynical. I did the same with my present situation and was, therefore, able to start thinking about what I might gain from my transitions work, even as it was becoming clear that I was fighting a losing leadership battle. And I did the same with my future by imagining a world in which I was guided by all the good I might do if I followed where my Orientation was leading. With just a little gratitude work, I was able to pull myself out of victimhood and into a world of possibilities.

SUMMARY

While our Orientation and our transitions may call us to develop new strengths, when we embark on leadership transitions, it's useful to remember the Resources that already serve us. Our Resources are the skills we've learned, the talents we've nurtured, and the character strengths that show up in our leadership. Each of these Resources enable us to shape the world around us. Each of them gives us the ability to leave our worlds better than how we found them. It's highly likely that most of them will continue to support us and our leadership no matter what circumstances we face.

Our Resources also include our sources of gratitude, a powerful tool for keeping our strengths focused on growth rather than just our protection. Gratitude, along with forgiveness, nudges us away from the negative emotion of victimhood toward the positive emotions of hope and possibility.

To explore your Resources, take some time to answer the following questions. It's useful to write in complete sentences, as if you are writing out a story rather than listing bullet points. Don't worry about how articulate your answers sound at first. Get something down. You can return to your answers for exploration later.

1. When the people around you compliment you on your strengths, what do they tell you? Think of the results of any recent performance appraisals or 360 feedback evaluations. What stands out? Which of these strengths have been most helpful to you in the course of your leadership? Which of them will be important during your transition? Which of them will you need the most to move in the direction of your Orientation?

2. Which of Seligman's 27 character strengths describe you well? Which have helped you most? Are there any character strengths that would be good for you to nurture in the course of your transition or in pursuit of your Orientation?

3. What are you most grateful for in your life and in your leadership? What would become possible if you remembered these sources of gratitude more often, and especially when you face chaotic times?

WRITING YOUR OWN (LEADERSHIP) STORY

> *The reason people find it so hard to be happy is that they always see the past better than it was, the present worse than it is, and the future less resolved than it will be.*

- MARCEL PAGNOL

Every transition is a step into chaos. Every step into chaos is an opportunity to explore what energizes us, think in new ways about the difference we want to make, and test our old ways of thinking and of being. Leadership transitions are no different. Every leadership transition holds the possibility of learning more about who we really are and who we really want to be. Every leadership transition gives us the opportunity to understand our elephants better, and help our elephants and our riders develop even greater harmony.

In Part One of *Leadership Transition*, I explained how our unconscious minds tend to work. I described how transitioning into the unknown can trigger all sorts of unconscious reflexes, including all our instincts associated with survival and self-preservation, with maintaining our status and security, with facing the fundamental anxieties of being human, with our shadows, even with how we write the core narratives of who we are and how the world works. Recognizing the triggers and exploring our reactions to them helps us bring unknown dimensions of our unconscious to consciousness. Exploring is how we bring our rider and our elephant together.

In Part Two, I described how our four core narratives provide us with strong guidance and a sturdy boat that keep us straight and true no matter how stormy the waters might be. I explained how the wise narrative of our Orientation provides us with clear direction. I described how the wise narrative of our Roots tells us how we want to live and how we want to lead. I shared how the wise narrative of our Relationships, especially our relationships with the people who secure us, with our organization and with our selves, helps ensure that we are nurturing the connections that matter the most. And I described how important the wise narrative of our Resources reminds us of all that we already have in us, that we are much stronger and more capable than we realize.

I'll close the book with a few reminders that integrate the spirit of the work. I'll include 11 of them, knowing that there's no particular magic to the number. I won't tell you that these are the 11 practices you need to follow on the way to leadership mastery. As I mentioned at the end of the introduction, this isn't that kind of book. I *will* tell you that they are all examples of the essence of deep leadership transitions work.

Before I turn to the 11, I want to share one last story with you. It's a story that describes the truest orientation of the work described in this book. The story takes place at the end of a leadership development program I'd helped to design and deliver a couple of years ago. The program was probably the first one that integrated the most important lessons from the research I describe in this book.

We were a group of about 20 leaders all working in the same global organization, along with me and a couple of wonderful facilitators who were supporting our work. It was the last session on the last day of the last module of the program. We travelled some interesting roads together, some easy, some hard, some expected and some surprising. We were well over the momentary glow of our early euphoria and into the *roll up our sleeves and let's see where this takes us* hard work of personal exploration. It was now time to express our thanks, share some memories of our work together over the previous year, talk about the highlights – maybe the personal work, or the secure-base leadership work we did on a rock wall outside of Chamonix with the help of a handful of local mountain guides, or the deep narrative work we did together in our small groups, seeing our stories interpreted through the eyes of the wise and wonderful people around us. Our last act together as a group was to stand in a circle and, one by one, share whatever needed to be shared, but always sharing the headline we wanted to give to our leadership stories.

Beautiful expressions of gratitude came out of the circle. Two expressions touched me especially deeply. One was from a participant, and one was from my elephant. When it came to her turn, the participant, Vicky, thanked the people around her. But she also thanked me, which I understood as an expression of gratitude toward the spirit of our work. She said, "From the beginning, from our first session together, it was clear that all you wanted to do was to get to know us, help us know ourselves and help us win." I love this feedback. I hope that *Leadership Transition* helps you in some small ways to know yourself better, and to win at life, leadership, self-discovery, and growth. We are all in a strange and wonderful game, and I wish for all of you to win your version of it.

The second touching expression came when it was my turn to share the headline of my leadership narrative. As usual, when presented with such opportunities, my elephant spoke up. It told the people in our little circle that the title of my leadership narrative is "*Beauty around every corner.*" I also wish you beauty around every corner of every transition that your life and your leadership give you. The treasures are there, even if sometimes we have to dig deep to find them.

My 11 practices for transitioning leaders follow. A warning up front: they aren't always easy practices. They *are* practices that often come up in our developmental work with transitioning leaders.

Homer, in The Odyssey, *the story about Odysseus' long journey home from the Trojan War, says,* "Even his griefs are a joy long after to one that remembers all that he wrought and endured." *Paul, in the Christian New Testament, says,* "We also rejoice in our sufferings, because we know that suffering produces perseverance; and perseverance, character." *An African proverb tells us that,* "Smooth seas do not make skillful sailors."

- LAWRENCE CALHOUN AND RICHARD TEDESCHI,
POSTTRAUMATIC GROWTH IN CLINICAL PRACTICE

I. LISTEN TO WHAT YOUR CHAOS IS TELLING YOU

Think of every step into the dangerous unknown as an act of poking the elephant. Remember that elephant language is the language of emotion. When your emotions speak up, listen to them. They are trying to tell you something. I remember when I was livid with anger during the worst days of my transition, and when I was afraid, defiant, sometimes feeling wise and righteous, sometimes childish, pointing at my enemies with all the black-and-white certainty that evolution gives us when we are under attack. It was difficult to look beneath the emotions for deeper meaning in the moment, although even in the most challenging moments, something inside of me caught glimpses of wisdom below the surface of my anger.

I've learned to ask myself three questions when I try to make sense of my emotions. The first question is, *"What is really going on here?"* It's a useful way to open up the elephant to curiosity when it is in full protective judgment mode. The question takes us beyond our instinctive and energetic reflexes against threats to our status, security, beliefs and values, core narratives and identity. It helps us detach and explore rather than just react. I've found it to be the first useful step in turning my intrusive narratives into intentional ones.

The second question is trickier, especially when our threat response levels are at their highest. The second intentional narrative question is, *"Am I doing anything to contribute to my own misery?"* In my darkest days, I would have raged against this question.[69] With some distance, I could ask myself with a clearer mind what about me made me vulnerable to the attacks I was experiencing. I could admit the limitations of my old approaches to leadership, my usual reliance on diplomacy, some ways in which I was naïve or immature, and how after so many years in the organization I had failed to properly protect myself. I wasn't willing to be dangerous. It was useful to understand all these nuances, remembering that good answers to our second question only come when it is asked with genuine curiosity rather than judgment.

The third intentional narrative question is, *"What wisdom can I take from this experience?"* Question two opens the door to learning. Question three steps into learning space and derives new, wiser narratives from the experience. For example, learning about the wisdom of balanced relationships with our employers, about the wisdom of our compass, about the importance of establishing a clear sense of the point of our leadership: these are all points of wisdom that I was able to take from research into my experience. You will have your own wiser narratives coming out of your transition narratives.

Sometimes our elephants don't like getting poked. Sometimes they've settled into a comfortable equilibrium. Sometimes we prefer forgetfulness-of-being to mindfulness-of-being because mindfulness-of-being is hard work. Listen to what your chaos is telling you anyway. If we pay attention to our emotions, we can usually find some deeper wisdom beyond them.

2. PAY ATTENTION TO YOUR COMPASS, ESPECIALLY WHEN IT'S DIFFICULT

As helpful as a well-developed and wise compass can be, our compass can also be annoying. Each of our four wise narratives calls us toward the highest version of ourselves. Sometimes it's an uncomfortable call. We tend to be comfortable in our old skins and with our usual behaviours. Our reflex to revert to our familiar ways is especially true when we feel that we are in danger. Under threat, we return to what we know. But pay attention to the call anyway. The discomfort brings a message. It is asking you to confront a part of you that might be getting in the way of your growth. In the early days of my own compass work, I was often annoyed with all that it was asking me to do – to be more honest with myself about a meaningful life and how I would need to grow to live it, to discard old beliefs, to put myself in an uncomfortable spotlight because that's what my compass asked me to do. Our compass asks us to confront uncomfortable truths about our old selves. There is wisdom in these confrontations. Jung famously wrote: "Where the fear, there is the task."[70] He wrote this in response to someone who was seeking guidance on how to deal with some old unresolved family losses. Not knowing the person's background, Jung replied with what he saw as a fundamental truth: growth is found in the direction of our fear.

The truth of the statement doesn't take away its discomfort. Here it's important to remember that your compass exists to serve you, not the other way around. If it makes you uncomfortable, it knows that its discomfort is in the service of your growth. We don't always need to follow our compass perfectly or feel guilty when we don't. As we will see in points three and 11, the compass isn't a tyrant. It is a friend who wants to help us grow.[71]

3. INVITE NEW WISDOM INTO YOUR COMPASS NARRATIVES

There's an interesting paradox that we need to manage when we do compass work. The paradox is that our compass is most useful when we are convinced by its wisdom, but if we set our narratives in stone, they become ideologies. The more certain we are of our compass, the more it steadies us. Until it becomes too certain, and then it limits us. Here we face the tyranny of too much order that we saw in Chapter 1. Ordering mechanisms are necessary in the face of life's chaos, but too much order becomes tyranny.

To avoid the tyranny of the compass, it's good to remember that our compass is always a distillation of our wisdom into four core narratives. As our wisdom grows, so too should our compass. When new experiences add to your experience and wisdom, this wisdom should be integrated into your compass narratives. This is why transitions bring such rich opportunities for compass work. Stepping into the unknown is a journey of wisdom-gathering.

Updating our compasses means reviewing them constantly to make sure that their wisdom still applies. It means asking yourself the questions at the end of each chapter in this book whenever you feel your compass may need a fresh look, and seeing how your new answers compare with your old ones. This isn't an easy exercise. Remember that we like to protect our core beliefs and assumptions because we rely on them so much. Every once in a while, though, it's good to take on the voluntary work of seeing if they still apply. Our leadership transitions give us a good excuse to see what new wisdom needs to come in, and what old wisdom has outlived its usefulness.

4. ALLOW YOUR ORIENTATION TO GUIDE YOUR DECISIONS, ESPECIALLY YOUR DECISIONS ABOUT HOW YOU SPEND YOUR TIME

I recently had a session with a new client who is preparing himself for a transition to an enterprise leadership role. He's a smart leader. He's navigated his way through a series of challenging transitions in his career and managed each one successfully. I noticed that as he was describing each transition, he always mentioned what he loved most about the new work. It seemed that he loved a lot, despite how challenging some of his transitions had been. Each transition had brought him fresh experience and new perspectives. He told all his stories clearly and quickly, with agile articulation.

When I asked him about what he wanted to explore in our work, he hesitated. For the first time in our conversation, he stumbled over his thoughts. He eventually said, "I feel like I should have a sense of purpose. I mean, how do I tell my wife and two kids the story about the difference I am making? What's the point of me? How do I know I am leading my good life? I feel like I need good answers to these questions."

The executive had a fantastic record of bringing order to chaotic leadership situations. He stumbled because the task he wants to take on is the hardest task of bringing order to his inner chaos. The challenge is that much harder because he is at the cusp of not only a leadership transition, but also the kind of life transition that we talked about in Chapters 2 and 4. He is at an age when questions of meaning at home and at work need to be answered. He understands that stepping into enterprise leadership means stepping away from his reflex to action so that he can guide others to action. He knows that he will be spending his time in a different way as he moves into his new role, and he wants a story of meaning to guide him along the way. Our Orientation gives us this North Star. It is the ultimate answer to the question of the point of us, at this time, in this chapter of our lives. Senior leaders find their Orientation to be most useful when it is reminding them of the deepest meaning of their lives and their work. It may not always be convenient to head in the direction of our Orientation, but it's always useful to have one. It's the only way we know that we are living a life of meaning through our work.

5. LET YOUR ROOTS TELL THE BEST STORY OF WHO YOU ARE

In Chapter 1, I described how uncomfortable it was for me to introduce myself after I left my old organization; my old labels didn't fit any more, I couldn't honestly describe myself as a senior executive, as an accomplished leader, as a member of my old organization's community. I had somehow lost the words to describe me, probably because I'd also lost a sense of who 'me' was.

Creating the wise narrative of my Roots helped me find new words. Now when I'm asked to introduce myself I usually start with the words of my Roots: *I believe that leadership is a rich laboratory for self-discovery and profound growth. I believe that organizational life often gets in the way of this essential journey. I believe that leaders can best take on the challenge of shaping organizations for the good once they've sorted out the chaos inside. I help them do that.* Being clear on my deepest beliefs and most essential values anchors me to my sense of me. Like our Orientation, our Roots can evolve. But in my experience, our Roots evolve more slowly. The beliefs and values that are truly critical to us tend to settle deeply and move carefully.

Given the importance of our Roots, it's useful to get in the habit of noticing how we are expressing them in our daily lives. Think of this practice as the Roots version of keeping our Orientation up to date. It's worth asking ourselves, once a week, once a month, how are my Roots showing up in the way I'm working? In the decisions I'm making? In how I am spending my time? Are my Roots evident in how I take on conflict? In how I treat people who annoy me? In whom I listen to and don't listen to? In whom I choose to spend my time with?

You'll have your own Roots questions to ask. It's important to know what your questions are. It's just as important to get into the habit of asking yourself your questions when you feel your Roots are being starved or uprooted to see what your honest answers tell you.

6. BECOME YOUR OWN SECURE BASE

Two relationships are worth constant nurturing: your relationship with one or two of your secure bases, and your relationship with yourself. No matter how long it might take for you to develop your connections with the few people whom you can depend upon for comfort and guidance, you can always work on your relationship with yourself.

As mentioned in Chapter 6, our relationship with ourselves is almost always complicated. The dynamics of it sit deep within our elephant. Carl Rogers' observations about how to care for ourselves as if we are worth growing are a good starting framework. So are the six secure base behaviours described in the chapter. A useful practice for becoming our own secure base is to combine the two. I usually frame this as combining the two into a single framework of seven questions. Ask yourself these questions at the end of every week, or (importantly) any time your critical inner voice holds you back rather than encouraging you forward. *1. Am I treating myself with unconditional positive regard? 2. Is my inner voice calm rather than strident? 3. Am I paying close attention to my thoughts and emotions? 4. Am I treating myself with the proper care? 5. Do I challenge myself in realistic and constructive ways? 6. Do I leverage all the wisdom I've learned over my many years of experience to guide myself through difficult circumstances? 7. Do I encourage myself, wholeheartedly and with all the positive emotion I deserve?*

It may feel more natural to practice our secure base leadership with the people we lead, but it is even more essential that we practice it on ourselves. What we learn from our self-practice we can extend to the people around us. The challenge is to make a habit out of asking ourselves the seven questions whenever we feel our inner energy becoming toxic rather than nourishing.

7. ACCEPT AND BE THANKFUL FOR THE GIFT OF YOUR RESOURCES

A frequent task in our transitions work is the task of helping leaders who have lost their confidence to regain it. It's a challenging task. Destabilizing experiences can wreck our sense that we really understand how the world works and how we should navigate our way through it. Once we've lost confidence in our old worldview, we might wonder why we should have any confidence in whatever we construct to replace it.

The task of regaining confidence isn't helped by our cultural emphasis on humility. Confidence can feel like arrogance, and it's possible, even probable, that we overemphasize humility to avoid appearing arrogant. Unfortunately, we tend to rely on unsophisticated definitions of humility when we manage ourselves between the humility–arrogance polarity.

The answer to accepting our strengths without leaning into arrogance is found in the beautiful outcome of post-traumatic growth research described in Chapter 7. Growth after trauma often comes in the form of a realization that we may be more vulnerable than we previously imagined, but we are also much stronger than we thought. Realizing our strengths isn't an expression of arrogance. It's an expression of profound wisdom. As much as we should always be aware of our own ignorance, we should just as often admit to the things in us that enable us to withstand life's many challenges and make the world around us just a little bit better. Our strengths are a gift we can give to the world. There's nothing wise about withholding our gifts. The world needs them.

It's useful to remind ourselves of our talents, skills and character strengths. Make a small list of five or six strengths that you feel are the critical Resources you bring to the pursuit of your Orientation. Ask yourself often if you've been expressing these gifts as much as you would like to. Ask yourself if your Orientation would be better served if you expressed them more. Acknowledge that wise humility is an understanding that we don't know far more than we know and that our mastery of life is always incomplete. But also acknowledge that your Orientation asks you to share your gifts freely, openly and enthusiastically.

8. PICK ONLY TWO OR THREE GROWTH GOALS AT A TIME

This growth practice reflects the reality of human capability. Conventional leadership development usually serves up a long list of rider-focused development targets. These are often skill-based targets, more cognitive than behavioural, and more transactional than practical.

It's fine to work on our leadership skills, but deep behavioural change comes from elephant work and our elephants respond best when we approach them with care and focus. If we take on too much elephant work at once, we will be tempted to look for easy surface-level answers to deeply embedded challenges. Remember that transformation only comes after confession, elucidation and education (see the end of *Origin Stories*, this book's introduction). Working effectively in elephant territory means committing to all four stages in the transformation process. Very few of us have the capability to take on this task for more than a few of our leadership dimensions.

The good news is that beneath-the-surface growth tends to have extraordinarily impactful results. Our elephants may be difficult to understand and even more difficult to guide, but when we do understand them and are able to guide them wisely in the service of our Orientation, they make an outsized difference. A good way to decide on which growth areas to commit to is to start with a long list, and then cull the list down according to three criteria: *1. Which growth areas have the greatest impact on my ability to lead in the direction of my Orientation? 2. Which growth areas will help me harmonize the four points of my compass? 3. Which growth areas scare me (see point 2 on this list)?* A recent client settled on two essential areas of personal exploration for her own development: the relationship between the part of her that valued personal power (agency) and the part of her that wants to belong to a tribe (communion), and her drive to push ahead when others fall behind. My own growth list during my leadership transition included learning how to express a wise and forceful warrior in the course of my work and understanding the main forces prodding my elephant when my values are assaulted. You'll have your own list, but make it a small one. Choosing the right few will make all the difference.

9. GROW, SLOWLY

Another seduction we sometimes face in our growth work is the fantasy that we can develop into an entirely new 'us.' We imagine a future us, and because the future us feels quite different than who we are today, we imagine that we need to take dramatic steps to get there. It's an understandable reflex, but there's a wise lesson to be taken from clinical work when it comes to personal growth: absent a crisis or trauma, growth happens best when it happens one small step at a time. Every step in the right direction, no matter how small, is a worthy step. This truth is especially important when we work in elephant territory and our elephant feels threatened. Gentle coaxing works better than dramatic action.

Two questions help us start on the journey to wise and realistic growth. The first question is: *What is my growth objective, really?* The second question is: *What small steps can I take in the direction of the growth I want to see in myself?*

I'll use a fresh example from my practice to illustrate the two questions. I worked with a functional executive a couple of years ago as part of a development program. Since the program, she has been promoted into regional leadership of her highly technical and vital function. There's a very good chance that her next transition will be into the global leadership of the function.

She's a determined, effective, personable and serious leader. I have no doubt that her technical expertise and humanity serve her beautifully. Her recent request to me was: How can I be more effective in the spotlight that my leadership now requires me to step into? She believes she is an effective presenter – at least this is the feedback she receives – but more and more she's required to step in front of larger groups of people to share her points of view.

We talked for a while about what success would look like for her. I was reassured when she answered that success wasn't really about her style on stage, but much more about how she managed her anxiety ahead of the event. "I'd be happy to be less terrified every time I step into the spotlight," she told me. I asked her if her hope was to get rid of her stage anxiety completely. I was reassured again when she said that tuning it down a little would also be a great result. So, rather than trying to turn a somewhat shy, thoughtful, studious and engaging leader into a stage entertainer (not who she is, and not who she wants to be), we are working on where her spotlight anxiety comes from, all the ways in which it serves her well, and how managing herself in the spotlight with a little less anxiety will enable her to lead in the direction of her Orientation more effectively. This kind of development is rooted in elephant work, and there are plenty of good initial small steps she can take to diminish her anxiety along the way.

10. MAKE TIME FOR YOUR SUPPORT SYSTEMS

Here I'm referring to all the activities and spaces that take you away from whatever intrusive thinking is impeding on your sense of inner equilibrium. Remember that chaos comes with the possibility of threat, threat activates unconscious protective mechanisms that often show up as negative emotion, and we turn negative emotion positive when we pivot away from intrusive rumination toward intentional rumination. The turn toward intentional rumination is less of a forced act than it is turning the mind away from its frantic thinking. A good first step to calming down our negative, protective inner chatter is to give it distance so that calmer, quieter emotions can enter into our inner space.

I've found a couple of helpful practices. Meditation can be useful if, and only if, your transition isn't taking you into trauma territory. Spending time in nature is becoming a well-documented calming practice. You might already have a collection of practices that bring you pleasure or joy outside of work. It doesn't really matter what they are, as long as they meet three criteria: 1. They take your mind away from whatever intrusive rumination you might be experiencing in the course of your transitions work; 2. You experience whatever stress the activity brings as positive stress; 3. They are the kind of activities you can and will make time for no matter how much time your transitions work is asking from you.

One CEO we work with makes time for a long swim every Thursday afternoon. Another frees up space every Friday morning for a long walk along the lakeshore close to his offices. A third makes sure she gets up to the mountains as often as possible, at least once a month, because being in the mountains allows her mind to drain away some of the work that calls for her attention during the course of a normal week. As with all our practices, this one needs to appeal to your individual circumstances, especially your sources of peace and joy. The challenge, typically, isn't in identifying your centring practices but rather in having the discipline to make time for them. Choose a few, and work hard to make time for them, especially if you feel you can't.

11. REMEMBER THAT YOUR LEADERSHIP IS, ABOVE ALL, A LABORATORY FOR SELF-EXPLORATION AND PERSONAL GROWTH

Finally, it's worth returning to a leadership frame that I introduced in Origin Stories. Your leadership is many things. It is a vocation, maybe a calling. It is how you pay the bills. It can provide security, a sense of success and status, a community. Your leadership can give you a sense of purpose in your life, a community, structure, a frame for how you think about yourself. It can and should be all these things. But it is also a laboratory for you to explore who you are, why you are that way, and who you want to become. Your leadership is an opportunity for you to test the answers you've created for some of the essential questions of your life. To explore how your instincts show up when you step into in-between space, how you deal with our deeply human anxieties associated with death, isolation, freedom and meaning, and how you find a truer you as you pass through different experiences and different ages. It is space for you to write and rewrite the essential narratives of you, of your purpose, your roots, your relationships and your strengths. And to keep striving for ever better narratives of who you are and the difference you want to make. As much as leadership is how we are useful in our world, it is also an exploration for who we really are, deeply, below the surface understanding of our cognitive mind. Step into the leadership laboratory with your own growth in mind and enjoy all the exploration and adventures you have along the way. If it's a strange and curious space, it's also a wonderful space for finding deep meaning and for making a profound difference.

NOTES

1. Murray Stein, *Transformation: Emergence of the Self* (College Station: Texas A&M University Press, 1998), 77–84. Stein's explanation of C. G. Jung's description of the process of personal transformation is a helpful reminder that deep transformation is both a necessary part of life and takes sustained effort.

2. Ervin Goffman, *Frame Analysis: An Essay on the Organization of Experience* (Boston: Northeastern University Press, 1986). If you don't mind heavy reading and you want to know more about our instinct for framing, try *Frame Analysis* for a deep dive into how we create mental schemas to organize how we think about the world so that we can engage in it with confidence. Goffman uses the example of theatre-going to explain primary frames. His thinking applies to how societies work, usually in terms of how a community's primary frames are shaped by cultural expectations. We translate the same very human model-making instinct to the world of psychology.

3. I'm betraying some modern cultural influences with these examples, but there's a reason our mythology and cultural story-telling so often tells the tale of the adventurous reordering of a system once chaos disrupts it. It's common in our mythology because it is the primary frame that we have used to make sense of our world through our evolution as a social species.

4. See Jordan B. Peterson, *Maps of Meaning: The Architecture of Belief* (New York: Routledge, 1999) for an exploration of how creativity in the space between order and chaos leads to meaning-making. Peterson provides a more accessible explanation in Jordan B. Peterson, *12 Rules for Life: An Antidote for Chaos* (Toronto: Random House Canada, 2018) but I used *Maps of Meaning* in my original research.

5. Yvon Chouinard, *let my people go surfing: The Education of a Reluctant Businessman* (New York: Penguin Books, 2016), 70. In this book, Chouinard tells the story of Patagonia's origins, early days, missteps and growth. It's an engaging tale of what it's like to follow your values when your values tell you to do things differently.

6. I'm stealing from the American Psychological Association's list here, and I notice how awkward I feel typing down some of its recommendations. As if 'developing self-confidence' is an easy thing to do. For the complete list, visit the APA's website, www.apa.org. If you have the time and the interest, read Boris Cyrulnik's fascinating work on the sources of resilience, including the story of how he became interested in the topic, in Boris Cyrulnick, *Resilience: How Your Inner Strength Can Set You Free from the Past* (London: Penguin, 2009).

7. See Jerome Bernstein, *Living in the Borderland: The Evolution of Consciousness and the Challenge of Healing Trauma* (New York: Routledge, 2005). Bernstein is a Jungian analyst. We explored some Jungian wisdom relating to transitional experiences in Chapter 2.

8. Carlo Strenger, *The Fear of Insignificance* (New York: Palgrave MacMillan, 2011), 35.

9. From Lawrence G. Calhoun and Richard G. Tedeschi, *Posttraumatic Growth in Clinical Practice* (New York: Routledge, 2013). Calhoun and Tedeschi's early clinical work in posttraumatic growth led the way to deep exploration of the mechanisms at play in psychological trauma. The chapters on wise narrative and on how to explore our narrative worlds draw from research that was encouraged by their work.

10. From Murray Stein, *The Principle of Individuation: Toward the Development of Human Consciousness* (Wilmette, Illinois: Chiron Publications, 2006), 72.

11. From Dan McAdams, *The Stories We Live By: Personal Myths and the Making of the Self* (New York: The Guilford Press, 1996), 259.

12. Jonathan Haidt, *The Happiness Hypothesis: Putting Ancient Wisdom and Philosophy to the Test of Modern Science* (London: Arrow Books, 2006). Haidt does a wonderful job of making profound research accessible and interesting.

13. Names and details are disguised.

14. Steven Pinker's fascinating exploration of how being human has changed over the past 200 years – a blink of the eye in evolutionary terms – is described in two recent books. In Steven Pinker, *The Better Angels of Our Nature* (London: Penguin Books, 2013), he shows how and why violence has diminished so dramatically over the past two centuries. In *Enlightenment Now* (London, Penguin Books, 2019), he explains how our turn toward reason, science, humanism and progress deserves much of the credit for why our lives are typically so much longer and more pleasant than the lives of even our most recent ancestors. In evolutionary terms, however, the rapid and dramatic increase in our lifespan poses a challenge: if our psychologies developed to help us survive until our children can protect themselves and have kids of their own – roughly to the age of 45, our average lifespan 200 years ago – how has it prepared us for the extra 35 years of life we suddenly have at our disposal?

15. Yes, some of us *do* like to put ourselves in danger, for complicated evolutionary reasons that include signaling our bravery and therefore raising our status within our community, and testing our ability to return safely from the limits of survivability. Read anything from evolutionary psychologist David Buss to dive into evolutionary explanations for patterns of behaviour that seem contrary to our survival instincts. For a review of evolutionary psychology try David M. Buss, *Evolutionary Psychology: The New Science of the Mind* (Boston: Pearson Education, Inc., 2004). For a fascinating exploration of how our deeply ingrained behavioural patterns show up in modern life, try David M. Buss, *The Murderer Next Door: Why the Mind Is Designed to Kill* (New York: The Penguin Press, 2005).

16. From *Buss, The Murderer Next Door: Why the Mind Is Designed to Kill.* I am struck by this observation whenever I encounter a leader who is struggling with being on the receiving end of humiliating behaviour. These leaders are typically burdened with two important tasks. They must sort out ways to prevent the behaviour from diminishing them, and they must resist the natural instinct to ease their humiliation by dominating someone else (see the next footnote).

17. From Robert M. Sapolsky, *Behave: The Biology of Humans at Our Best and Worst* (London: Vintage, 2017), Every time we lose a battle in work or in life, our instinct is to compensate by seeking out and winning a battle against a weaker opponent. Bullying flows downward.

18. See Richard Dawkins, *The Selfish Gene* (New York: Oxford University Press, 1976). This classic in evolutionary psychology is a good introduction to the field.

19. Irvin Yalom and Rollo May were my entry points into existential psychology. Anything by either of them is worth reading. See Irvin Yalom, *Love's Executioner and Other Tales of Psychotherapy* (New York: Basic Books, 1989), *Existential Psychotherapy* (London: Basic Books, 1980), and *The Gift of Therapy* (New York: HarperCollins, 2009) for good primers in the subject. Each one helped me to understand how existentialism might be important for transitioning leaders. Carlo Strenger's *The Fear of Insignificance: Searching for Meaning in the Twenty-First Century* was a useful modern take on how existentialism applies to our current cultural challenges. As you will see, meaning is an essential idea for the existentialists. As you will also see, it is just as essential an idea for leaders who hope to navigate their way through chaos of leadership transitions.

20. Here's an interesting observation: "Research suggests strangers read each other's thoughts and feelings with an accuracy of just 20%. Friends and lovers? A mere 35%." That's how alone we are: no matter how well I think I know my wife, after almost 15 years of marriage I can guess what is running through her mind with decent accuracy about a third of the time. From Will Storr, *The Science of Storytelling* (London: William Collins, 2019), 37.

21. We see the theme of specialness play out when we work with executives who are edging up to their retirement. The question they often try to answer isn't so much, *"What will I do next?"* but rather, *"How can I still be special in the next chapter of my life?"* It's a difficult question to answer if leadership is the only source of specialness in the executive's life.

22. In their clinical research into organizational mobbing, Maureen Duffy and Len Sperry note how devastated leaders are when they realize how quickly they can be abandoned by trusted colleagues when the support of those colleagues is needed most. Their work is a helpful reminder of just how powerful our need for community is, and just how painful it can be when that community disappears. See Maureen Duffy and Len Sperry, *Mobbing: Causes, Consequences and Solutions* (New York: Oxford University Press, 2012) and Maureen Duffy and Len Sperry, *Overcoming Mobbing: A Recovery Guide for Workplace Aggression and Bullying* (New York: Oxford University Press, 2014).

23. Carlo Strenger outlines the fundamentals of existential psychology in Carlo Strenger, *The Fear of Insignificance: Searching for Meaning in the Twenty-first Century.* Strenger focuses this work on the challenges of finding deeper meaning when our cultures increasingly encourage shallow alternatives. He mentions what other clinical schools of psychology also observe: we tend to protect our sources of psychological comfort vigorously, even if we suspect that they are a poor substitute for more mindful work. See the chapter on trauma..

24. I recently had a session with a new CEO. He loves the work, and he is very, very good at it. He is calm, thoughtful, interested, serious, open, curious: all the things you'd hope for in someone who is steering the ship through challenging waters. Toward the end of our discussion, he mentioned something that had been bothering him. We had already talked about the enormous weight of activity that he'd faced over the previous three months. He was prepared for the firehose of work that needed to be done. But the thing that had been bothering him wasn't this. At the end of our conversation, he asked, "Why is it that at 50 years old, with the career that I've had and with the work that I love, I still depend on the praise of others to feel good about myself." That's an elephant question. It's common territory for leaders of that age. More on how we find answers to these kinds of questions in Part Two.

25. Calhoun and Tedeschi, *Posttraumatic Growth in Clinical Practice* (2013), 22. This work and their *Handbook of Posttraumatic Growth: Research and Practice* (New York: Psychology Press, 2014) are two remarkable explorations of the emerging field in posttraumatic growth. The 2013 work is an easier read and a useful introduction into how some people can turn even their most challenging experiences into profound and positive personal growth.

26. The list of beliefs feels naïve when I read it now, and I remember how strongly I reacted when someone pointed out my naivete. He was right, but our minds can be more hopeful than rational when they construct our core beliefs.

27. This list of core assumptions comes from clinical practitioner and researcher Ronnie Janoff-Bulman. Professor Janoff-Bulman's trauma work has been an essential contribution toward understanding the importance of stable mental schemas for keeping us feeling safe and in control of our worlds. The confusion that comes when our core schemas are destroyed is at the heart of trauma. See Ronnie Janoff-Bulman, *Shattered Assumptions: Towards a New Psychology of Trauma* (New York: The Free Press, 1992).

28. As always, certain details of these stories have been altered to honour confidentiality, but the essence of each story comes from actual cases.

29. Calhoun and Tedeschi, *Posttraumatic Growth in Clinical Practice*. Early in their book, Calhoun and Tedeschi describe this research pivot from resilience to growth.

30. Bernstein, *Living in the Borderland*. By sacred trauma, Bernstein refers to the curious fact that in some cases, trauma sufferers recognize that the growth opportunities that can come from destructive experiences are so valuable they are worth the suffering.

31. Bessel van der Kolk, *The Body Keeps the Score: Brain, Mind and Body in the Healing of Trauma* (New York: Penguin Books, 2015).Van Der Kolk's work is a useful read for anyone who wants to understand the psychological mechanisms that come into play – and stay in play, if we let them – when we experience massive personal destabilization.

32. I've adapted this illustration from Calhoun and Tedeschi, *The Handbook of Posttraumatic Growth*, 8. My adaptation includes many of their process steps but integrates the kinds of forces that leaders are likely to face in the course of their transitional work.

33. Ash's story of using her struggles to find new meaning in her work follows a common theme in personal growth. We often find fresh meaning by helping others deal with the same struggles we've had to overcome. Calhoun and Tedeschi tell a few of these stories from their clinical work. Writer and journalist David Brooks recently collected a book's worth of these stories in a wonderful exploration of how the pivot away from self-importance toward positive impact is often at the heart of the wisest personal narratives. See David Brooks, *The Road to Character* (New York: Random House, 2015).

34. From Calhoun and Tedeschi, *Posttraumatic Growth in Clinical Practice*. Calhoun and Tedeschi describe the common manifestations of growth in clinical practice in the book's first chapter.

35. From Calhoun and Tedeschi, *Posttraumatic Growth in Clinical Practice*, 9. The authors make an interesting connection between emotional openness and compassion. It may be that the more open we are with our emotions, the more deeply we understand them. The more deeply we understand them in ourselves, the more we are able to understand the emotions that may be at the root of the behaviours of the people around us, including the behaviours that typically come from suffering. See Chapter 9 of Steven Pinker, *The Better Angels of Our Nature* (2011) for an exhaustive investigation of the role compassion plays in explaining the remarkable decrease in violence we've experienced in our societies over recent generations.

36. The strong emotion came from a part of me that wanted to fight and was tired of being restrained. I'd built a successful career through diplomacy and by not taking office politics too seriously. I avoided conflict, and so when conflict came that I couldn't avoid, I struggled. The wisdom I took from the emotion was that, in some cases, you must fight. Learning how to fight well - to have a useful monster inside of you, as some psychologists would say - is an important skill.

37. Calhoun and Tedeschi, *Posttraumatic Growth in Clinical Practice*, 10.

38. Calhoun and Tedeschi, *Posttraumatic Growth in Clinical Practice*, 10–11.

39. See Jeffrey Pfeffer, *Dying for a Paycheck: How Modern Management Harms Employee Health and Company Performance - and What We Can Do About It* (New York: HarperCollins, 2018) for research into the dangers of the modern workplace. In recent years Switzerland, my home for the past three decades, has experienced high profile cases of suicide by senior leaders in two of our most well-known organizations.

40. Calhoun and Tedeschi, *Posttraumatic Growth in Clinical Practice*, 12.

41. Calhoun and Tedeschi, *Posttraumatic Growth in Clinical Practice*, 12.

42. Viktor E. Frankl, *Man's Search for Meaning: An Introduction to Logotherapy* (New York: Touchstone, 1959), 12.

43. See Erik H. Erikson, *Childhood and Society* (New York: W. W. Norton & Company, 1950). The conflict of Stage Seven is successfully resolved when the individual feels that he or she is contributing to the world, through family and through work. Stagnation happens when we haven't found a way to make a meaningful difference. When we stagnate, we lose a sense of our own significance and pull back from our engagement with the world. The resolution of conflict of the next and final stage, which Erikson called *Integrity vs Despair*, comes when we can look back at our lives with a sense of satisfaction with a life well-lived.

44. Huston Smith, *The World's Religions: Our Great Wisdom Traditions* (New York: PerfectBound, 2003), Location 1158

45. I could have written that I was not quite myself. This sense of 'I'm not myself' is a common psychological reaction from people who've been shaken by a profoundly disturbing experience. I mentioned at the start of this book that after one senior leader shared the story of his leadership trauma with me, his wife mentioned, "He was possessed. He wasn't himself. He was possessed by something." Clinical work would say that we are possessed by a sometimes overwhelming confusion that comes when our core narrative structures fail in the face of experience.

46. There's a quotation that's sometimes attributed to Carl Jung, founder of analytical psychology, and sometimes to Joseph Campbell, who studied mythology, and especially the archetypal mythologies that seem to appear in different forms around the world. The comment's wisdom is to point out the importance of remaining deeply curious about our Orientation, even when we are comfortable with it, so that we avoid adapting someone else's. See Joseph Campbell, *Pathways to Bliss: Mythology and Personal Transformation* (Novato, California: New World Library, 2004).

47. All quotations here are taken from Calhoun and Tedeschi, *Posttraumatic Growth in Clinical Practice*, 10–11.

48. The quality of our Relationships is important enough to justify its own point on the Leader's Compass.

49. McAdams, *The Stories We Live By*, 75. Early in the book, McAdams explores how our personal myth-making evolves at different stages in our lives.

50. By way of example, the following five beliefs came out of a conversation I had with a senior leader who was doing a remarkable job of maintaining his calmness in the face of extraordinary business chaos: 1. Never give up. Persistence in the pursuit of the right goals is almost always necessary; 2. Right is right, and wrong is wrong. Don't convince yourself otherwise just because doing the right thing is difficult; 3. Fortune favours the brave. Courage is necessary to overcome our obstacles; 4. Focus relentlessly on what you can influence. Don't get distracted by what you can't; 5. Seniority in the hierarchy doesn't stop me from telling the truth as I see it. People higher in the hierarchy shouldn't be protected from difficult truths.

51. The definition is from Duffy and Sperry, *Mobbing: Causes, Consequences, and Solutions*. Ash was describing her experience of being mobbed when she told me her leadership story.

52. Duffy and Sperry, *Mobbing: Causes, Consequences, and Solutions*, 169.

53. These examples are taken from Calhoun and Tedeschi, *Posttraumatic Growth in Clinical Practice*, 9.

54. Calhoun and Tedeschi, *Posttraumatic Growth in Clinical Practice*, 9

55. Most of the academic work I used in my research into attachment theory and its importance for how we deal with transitions in life comes from two works: John Bowlby, *A Secure Base: Parent-Child Attachment and Healthy Human Development* (New York: Basic Books, 1988), and Jeremy Holmes, *The Search for the Secure Base: Attachment Theory and Psychotherapy* (New York, Routledge, 2001).

56. I am integrating two schools of psychology here. The first is transactional analysis (TA), a way of framing relationships between humans that was explored and developed by Eric Berne, a Canadian psychiatrist. See Eric Berne, *Games People Play: The Psychology of Human Relationship* (New York: Grove Press, 1964). Berne describes the healthy and unhealthy ways that the parent-child dynamic shows up in our relationships. I bring in the dramatically named concept of terror management theory (TMT) to explain our reflex to please first our parents and then our culture to mitigate our fear of death. For an excellent explanation of the death-mitigating reflexes that might be sitting within our elephants see Sheldon Solomon, Jeff Greenberg and Tom Pyszczynski, *The Worm at the Core: On the Role of Death in Life* (New York: Random House, 2015). Their work explores territory first covered in Ernest Becker, *The Denial of Death* (London: Souvenir Press, 1973), a work that won Becker the Pulitzer Prize.

57. Our deep drive for status is well-documented. Steven Pinker refers to it as an adaptive reflex (see Steven Pinker, *How The Mind Works* (New York: W. W. Norton and Company, 1997)). David M. Buss notes at length its evolutionary importance (see Buss, *The Murderer Next Door: Why the Mind Is Designed to Kill* (2004) and Buss, *Evolutionary Psychology: The New Science of the Mind* (2005). Will Storr tells the story of our evolutionary need for status in layman's language in Will Storr, *The Status Game: On Human Life and How to Play It* (London: HarperCollins, 2021).

58. All lessons are taken from Carl. R. Rogers, *On Becoming a Person – A Therapist's View of Psychotherapy* (New York: Houghton Mifflin Company, 1961). Rogers describes them in Part 1 of the book: "This is me."

59. From Calhoun and Tedeschi, *Posttraumatic Growth in Clinical Practice*, 7–8.

60. Seligman was a driving force behind the development of positive psychology. For a thorough classification of positive aspects of human behaviour, see Christopher Peterson and Martin E. P. Seligman, *Character Strengths and Virtues: A Handbook and Classification* (New York: Oxford University Press, 2004). If ever you want to understand the dimensions of character that deserve your attention, you won't find a much better guide than this. For the main concepts of positive psychology and an excellent primer on the topic, see Martin E. P. Seligman, *Authentic Happiness: Using the New Positive Psychology to Realize Your Potential for Deep Fulfillment* (London: Nicholas Brealey Publishing, 2002).

61. Seligman, *Authentic Happiness* dives into each of the components of the formula in detail. I'm drawing from Chapter Four here.

62. Seligman, *Authentic Happiness*, 61.

63. Seligman, *Authentic Happiness*, 260.

64. Seligman, *Authentic Happiness*, 137.

65. Seligman, *Authentic Happiness*, 137.

66. Seligman, *Authentic Happiness* lists 24 strengths, but in the original work described in Peterson and Seligman, *Character Strengths and Virtues*, the authors include more. I went with the longer list.

67. David Denborough, *Retelling the Stories of Our Lives: Everyday Narrative Therapy to Draw Inspiration and Transform Experience* (New York: W. W. Norton& Company, 2014).

68. From McAdams, *The Stories We Live By*. Readers who are familiar with Jungian archetypes might notice similarities between archetypes and McAdams' imagoes. Both are helpful. Archetypes – genetically imbedded patterns of behaviour that exist within us all because of their usefulness to our survival – enabled me to imagine different characters that might be playing oversized and undersized roles on my inner. Two archetypes, the Warrior and the Lover, fit neatly into McAdams' agentic and communal polarity. I appreciate McAdams' work with imagoes because it encourages us to explore our inner characters in personal terms.

69. This question is *not* encouraging you to blame yourself for whatever chaos you might be in. A common reflex in the face of difficult circumstances is to blame ourselves. We often prefer to blame ourselves than to admit that we are just as vulnerable to life's randomness as anyone else: self-blame is a well-documented trauma response. I blamed myself for most of my difficulties during my transition, at least until I described my situation to a professional body psychotherapist. When I told him about the people I was fighting, he said, "They sound like narcissistic perverts." I asked him what one does when one is battling a couple of narcissistic perverts. "Run," he said. "They're good at it, they leave destruction in their wake wherever they go, you won't be able to fight them unless you become like them, and the point of it for them is to cause pain." I understood a little better that the situation I was in had more to do with some of the people around me than any tragic flaw in my own character. But I also understood that there were things I could learn to avoid getting myself into similar situations in the future.

70. *Letters of C. G. Jung: Volume 2*, 1951-1961

71. See also Barbara Turner-Vesselago, *Writing Without a Parachute: The Art of Freefall* (London: Jessica Kingsley Publishers, 2013). Turner-Vesselago mentions what she playfully calls the Five Precepts for open and honest self-exploration through writing. Precept Four is *"Go where the energy is, or go fearward. As you write, be aware of moving toward whatever feels most charged to you. If several things come up at once, choose one that strikes you most forcefully, whether you're attracted or repelled. And if you're still not sure, choose the one you're most afraid to write about. Go fearward."*

BIBLIOGRAPHY

Becker, Ernest. *The Denial of Death*. London: Souvenir Press, 1973.

Berne, Eric. *Games People Play: The Psychology of Human Relationship*. New York: Grove Press, 1964.

Bernstein, Jerome. *Living in the Borderland: The Evolution of Consciousness and the Challenge of Healing Trauma.* New York: Routledge, 2005.

Bowlby, John. *A Secure Base: Parent-Child Attachment and Healthy Human Development*. New York: Basic Books, 1988.

Brooks, David. *The Road to Character*. New York: Random House, 2015.

Buss, David M. *Evolutionary Psychology: The New Science of the Mind*. Boston: Pearson Education, Inc., 2004.

Buss, David M. *The Murderer Next Door: Why the Mind Is Designed to Kill*. New York: The Penguin Press, 2005.

Calhoun, Lawrence G., and Richard G. Tedeschi, *Posttraumatic Growth in Clinical Practice.* New York: Routledge, 2013.

Calhoun, Laurence G., and Richard G. Tedeschi, *Handbook of Posttraumatic Growth: Research and Practice.* New York: Psychology Press, 2014.

Campbell, Joseph. *Pathways to Bliss: Mythology and Personal Transformation*. Novato, California: New World Library, 2004.

Chouinard, Yvon. *Let My People Go Surfing: The Education of a Reluctant Businessman*. New York: Penguin Books, 2016.

Cyrulnick, Boris. *Resilience: How Your Inner Strength Can Set You Free from the Past*. London: Penguin, 2009.

Dawkins, Richard. *The Selfish Gene*. New York: Oxford University Press, 1976.

Denborough, David. *Retelling the Stories of Our Lives: Everyday Narrative Therapy to Draw Inspiration and Transform Experience*. New York: W. W. Norton & Company, 2014.

Duffy, Maureen, and Len Sperry, *Mobbing; Causes, Consequences and Solutions.* New York: Oxford University Press, 2012.

Duffy, Maureen, and Len Sperry, *Overcoming Mobbing: A Recovery Guide for Workplace Aggression and Bullying.* New York: Oxford University Press, 2014.

Erikson, Erik H. *Childhood and Society.* New York: W. W. Norton & Company, 1950.

Frankl, Viktor E. *Man's Search for Meaning: An Introduction to Logotherapy.* New York: Touchstone, 1959.

Goffman, Ervin. *Frame Analysis: An Essay on the Organization of Experience.* Boston: Northeastern University Press, 1986.

Haidt, Jonathan. *The Happiness Hypothesis: Putting Ancient Wisdom and Philosophy to the Test of Modern Science.* London: Arrow Books, 2006.

Holmes, Jeremy. *The Search for the Secure Base: Attachment Theory and Psychotherapy.* New York, Routledge, 2001.

Janoff-Bulman, Ronnie. *Shattered Assumptions: Towards a New Psychology of Trauma.* New York: The Free Press, 1992.

Jung, C. G. *The Letters of C. G. Jung, Volume 2, 1951-1961.* London: Routledge, 1976.

McAdams, Dan. *The Stories We Live By: Personal Myths and the Making of the Self.* New York: The Guilford Press, 1996.

Peterson, Christopher, and Martin E. P. Seligman, *Character Strengths and Virtues: A Handbook and Classification.* New York: Oxford University Press, 2004.

Peterson, Jordan B. *Maps of Meaning: The Architecture of Belief.* New York: Routledge, 1999.

Pfeffer, Jeffrey. *Dying for a Paycheck: How Modern Management Harms Employee Health and Company Performance – and What We Can Do About It.* New York: HarperCollins, 2018.

Pinker, Steven. *The Better Angels of Our Nature.* London: Penguin Books, 2013.

Pinker, Steven. *Enlightenment Now.* London, Penguin Books, 2019.

Pinker, Steven. *How The Mind Works.* New York: W. W. Norton and Company, 1997.

Rogers, Carl R. *On Becoming a Person – A Therapist's View of Psychotherapy.* New York: Houghton Mifflin Company, 1961.

Sapolsky, Robert M. *Behave: The Biology of Humans at Our Best and Worst.* London: Vintage, 2017.

Seligman, Martin E. P. *Authentic Happiness: Using the New Positive Psychology to Realize Your Potential for Deep Fulfillment.* London: Nicholas Brealey Publishing, 2002.

Smith, Huston. *The World's Religions: Our Great Wisdom Traditions.* New York: PerfectBound, 2003.

Solomon, Sheldon, Jeff Greenberg and Tom Pyszczynski, *The Worm at the Core: On the Role of Death in Life.* New York: Random House, 2015.

Stein, Murray. *The Principle of Individuation: Toward the Development of Human Consciousness.* Wilmette, Illinois: Chiron Publications, 2006.

Stein, Murray. *Transformation: Emergence of the Self.* College Station: Texas A&M University Press, 1998.

Storr, Will. *The Science of Storytelling.* London: William Collins, 2019.

Storr, Will. *The Status Game: On Human Life and How to Play It.* London: HarperCollins, 2021.

Strenger, Carlo. *The Fear of Insignificance.* New York: Palgrave MacMillan, 2011.

Turner, Victor. *The Ritual Process: Structure and Anti-Structure.* New York: Routledge, 1969.

Turner-Vesselago, Barbara. *Writing Without a Parachute: The Art of Freefall.* London: Jessica Kingsley Publishers, 2013.

van der Kolk, Bessel. *The Body Keeps the Score: Brain, Mind and Body in the Healing of Trauma.* New York: Penguin Books, 2015.

van Gennep, Arnold. *The Rites of Passage.* Chicago: University of Chicago Press, 1960.

Woodman, Marion, and Elinor Dickson. *Dancing in the Flames: The Dark Goddess in the Transformation of Consciousness.* Toronto: A. A. Knopf, 1996.

Yalom, Irvin. *Love's Executioner and Other Tales of Psychotherapy.* New York: Basic Books, 1989.

Yalom, Irvin. *Existential Psychotherapy.* London: Basic Books, 1980.

Yalom, Irvin. *The Gift of Therapy.* New York: HarperCollins, 2009.